the Cocktail Hour in Jackson Hole

the Cocktail Hour in Jackson Hole

By Donald Hough

Illustrated by Howard Willard

HIGH PLAINS PUBLISHING COMPANY, INC.

Special thanks is given Floy Tonkin, publisher of the Jackson Hole Guide, Jackson, Wyoming, for permission to reprint several of these chapters.

Library of Congress Catalog Card Number: 93-77110

ISBN 1-881019-02-0

High Plains Publishing Company, Inc.
Post Office Box 1860
Worland, Wyoming 82401

The dedication of a book is a private and personal thing, an old-fashioned gesture which, like the horse, long ago should have passed into limbo. However, here is a blank page, set aside for the author, which in this case means me. Nobody reads it.

This small book is addressed to many people in Jackson Hole, perhaps to all of them, with infinite thanks. It also is addressed to the Bridal Shop of Ohrbach's store in New York City, in which my wife's effort, reflected by her charming assistants, has made the writing of it financially possible.

As to the actual dedication, there is no point in my wasting time even thinking about it because the answer is as sharp and clear now as it has been since the beginning.

TO BERRY
my lovely wife.

Contents

the Cocktail Hour in Jackson Hole

Part I. THE HOUR ITSELF

chapter I

Anybody for a Drink?

THE COCKTAIL hour, an institution now fully integrated into the basic pattern of our extracurricular life—in some of its manifestations tending even to be curricular—through a curious distortion of history is thought of not only as belonging mostly to the larger cities and the environs thereof, especially those in the East, but as an urban invention from the start.

This fallacy readily can be handled by any serious student of the American scene. The Westerner, who is a serious student of this scene by right of eminent domain, his roots in it being deeper than those found in any other region, can convince you in a matter of weeks that the cocktail hour was introduced by Coronado and De Soto, who brought it in from Europe long before the Pilgrims came up with the cold turkey sandwich, then was picked up by Lewis & Clark, later improved upon by the Indians, and brought to full flower under the delicate nursing of the United States cowboy.

This lovely hour reached its early peak along the line of the shifting terminals of the Chisholm Trail and its variations in, of all places, the state of Kansas. The towns of Abilene, Wichita, Hays City, Ellsworth, and Dodge City each served, in turn, as railhead shipping points for cattle driven up from Texas, a job that took three months at least, with no coffee breaks en route. At these trail-ends there were many hearty meetings—not quite as hearty as Metro-Goldwyn-Mayer and associates endlessly suggest, but often exuberant—both unilaterally between the trail drivers themselves and between these and last year's friends in town, supposing them still to be alive.

Here the cocktail hour, along with a tightly condensed version called the cocktail party, was nailed to the mast with an impact that was reflected in the fact that Kansas became—as it still remains—a bulwark of dry sentiment in the United States when the farmers from points eastward, being on the nonwhoopee side by nature, and having no time for anything that could not be used for fertilizer, moved in and took a dim view of what was going on.

The last of the Kansas joints to be closed was Dodge City, circa 1885, for the final trail drives ended here. From that point the cattlemen, with a quick one for the road, retreating in good order before the relentless march of the farmers, took their herds into the Western hills, which were okay for cattle but no good for wheat. They, or rather their descendants, are in the mountains today, where in spite of a heavy infiltration of dudes, tourists, roving schoolteachers on vacation and other minor-league adventurerers they carry on both the cocktail hour and the industry that spawned it.

However, there is one large difference between the correct Western version of the hour and the Eastern, or large city, corruption of it. In New York (which I intend as a generic term covering all big centers of urban population, no matter where they are) it is a two-hour interlude, roughly from five to seven.* In the mountain country it spreads itself over more than two months, roughly from mid-September until Thanksgiving or thereabout—although in any case you always have to allow for those who suffer from a chronic salty stomach and show up early with their tongues in their teeth and certain lonely souls who can't stand solitude and insist upon carrying on after hours: in New York until dawn, in the West until March or until jail, whichever comes first.

This difference in approach to the timing and duration of the hour is fundamental and natural. It is supposed to be a pause for social intercourse, in the interest of relaxation from tension, among friends and other likely-looking babes when work is done, and whether a man's labor is counted on a daily basis or in terms of longer periods it's all of a piece. In the city a man works, or puts up as good a show as he can manage, from nine until five, with a few hours off for lunch; out in the distant hills a fellow is more likely to think of his efforts in terms of months, or seasons, or a year.

This is especially true in places like Jackson Hole, Wyoming . . .

The Hole is an isolated valley of dramatic beauty cupped high in the backbone of the Rockies and surrounded by them, accessible only by roads, all of which are long and tough. Without counting the mountains that rise on all sides around it, it is from eight to fifteen miles wide and about forty long. Its bottomlands, the precious winter cattle range, above which tower lush summer pastures in the public domain, long ago were settled by homesteading stockmen.

* The Old Reliable Café, 755 Third Ave., SE corner of 47th Street, Manhattan, has a legend painted on its brick wall, 47th Street side, that says in very large letters COCKTAIL HOUR, 2–4 PM. Although the Old Reliable, dating back more than half a century, is not heavily patronized by what ordinarily is thought of as the cocktail crowd, the management claims that this jump on its competitors has paid off, over the years.

Although it still is a fairly important producer of beef, the complexion of the Hole in late years has changed a lot, particularly during the summer months.

It lies just south of Yellowstone Park, and the relatively new Grand Teton National Park now covers the more spectacular parts of it. As a consequence of this situation an enormous number of outlanders swarm in over the mountain passes, in season, driving their cars with one hand and holding their mouths open with the other.

These people have to be processed, the same as any herd has to be. This means that much of the valley's permanent personnel, as we used to call it in the Army, is pretty well scattered through it in the summer, now not only tending cattle on the high ranges but nursing dudes and tourists everywhere, on all ranges including the indoor ones, while at the same time the home guard left in Jackson, only town in the Hole (Pop. 1,239), is up to its collective neck in these automotive hordes from behind the Granite Curtains that flank it.

All hands eagerly await relief from these exhausting—if highly remunerative—duties, and as August wanes their thoughts turn in mass unanimity to Labor Day, after which they can get together among themselves as dignified and independent adult citizens of the Republic, their hair free of New Yorkers (generic term), and in renewed friendship and shared experience toss a quick one or sip a tall one against the rigors of the impending winter.

Labor Day is not significant because it marks the end of one season and the beginning of another, for it has no place in the equinoctial scheme of things, but because of its arbitrary place on the workaday calendar by which the country as a whole, especially the rest of the country, goes about its business: vacations are over, the children must get back to school, the dreadful films must be developed in time to bore one's friends through the winter, old desks and new bills must be faced, and so must Christmas, the next financial holocaust. The footloose schoolteachers after a happy time in Jackson Hole have to put up their hair, fall out of love with the cowboys, throw away their pants, and otherwise prepare themselves for the personal hobbles imposed upon them by the home-town Parent-Teacher Association, and face the professional realities of the eternal blackboard . . .

So it is time for the rich visitors, ever welcome at the cash register, to be on their way, and the outbound cars zip past in staccato farewell as they hurtle over the passes and through the canyons in a clap of noxious fumes.*

Now begins, quietly at first, but with ever-mounting fervor and noise, the enveloping movement of the permanent personnel toward Jackson, while in the town itself shoulders and nerves droop a little in pleasant relaxation as sighs of relief whisper sweet nothings to each other and old friends find time to exchange greetings, neighbor to rediscover neighbor, everybody surprised to find that everybody else looks only a few months older, after all.

The cowboys start to move their charges down from the summer range; the dude wranglers, having muttered the last of their private imprecations, at long last can drop their Hollywood lingo and speak normally; the Park Rangers have given their last tired talks on the Wonders of Nature and have packed their magic-lantern slides away in sheets of

* Throughout, I speak of "dudes and tourists." There is a difference. A dude is one who comes in for weeks or months, stays at a dude ranch or something like it, dresses more like a cowhand than a cowhand does, rides horses, and in a kind of simple-minded way tries to fit into the country. The dude is in the minority; he, and especially she, takes up very little space except when sitting down. A tourist is just a tourist, absorbed in the intricacies of the Dynaflow Drive, buying picture postcards so that when he gets home he can see where he has been.

used mimeograph paper for the winter. The Forest Service people have warned about cigarette butts and picnic fires for the last time this year and outlying gas stations and roadside lunchrooms have been boarded up to await the next harvest.

So the clan gathers . . .

The trappers, the remote ranchers—both dude and cattle—the government men of various kinds from outlying stations, and others difficult precisely to classify, come in to stock up for the winter, which is very long, very cold, and often paralyzes the valley with its blizzards and with snows that can reach up to fifteen feet on the level, without drifting. Some of the ranchers move into town so their kids can go to high school, there to learn all about the Italian Renaissance or to memorize the date of the Battle of Tours (A.D. 732).

In a word, the cocktail hour is here.

The small public square—or, rather, the complex of business establishments that surround it—takes the main impact, with the four bars, assisted by the Elks' Club, handling most of the load. Although there are some parties and family gatherings in private homes, most of the celebrants drift toward these public precincts just because it is an old Western custom, particularly at this time of year. The upvalley people and the downvalley people who are in for shopping, for example, leave their accumulated purchases in the bars, to be picked up later—or leave husbands or wives, to be picked up later, or their small children, evidently, so the bartenders swear, to be picked up in the spring.

I remember Willard Miner, a bachelor of the old school, as good a bartender and as poor a baby-sitter as ever lived, driven almost out of his wits by this last dreadful chore, giving the little nuisances a half jigger of gin, laced with bar syrup, when they began to yowl.

Above and beyond these relatively solid citizens of course

are the free-lancers who come to town for no other purpose than to have a few drinks with their friends.

In any case each bartender now serves as a personal clearinghouse for information, advice, and counsel of all kinds, with emphasis on the movements, whereabouts, and condition of everybody in town, or even out of town, no matter how fast the scene changes. And when things really are humming this can change with the speed of light, especially with respect to the more complicated situations.

Everybody seems to be looking for everybody else, and the bartender is up against the delicate chore of sorting out these requests and deciding, with split-second timing, when to nod and when to shake his head, either according to his own judgment or because he has been briefed ahead of time. He must be careful, when last night's heavy celebrant shows up the next day with his wife, to greet him as though he hadn't seen him for a coon's age—at the same time watching for a signal that the guy has come in to prove that he was there last night, not someplace else, thus adding to the trials of the hard-working man behind the mahogany in his endeavor to keep things sorted out and in some kind of order, trying to remember everything, to forget everything, to please everybody, and to come up to Thanksgiving with a whole skin himself.

The bars in Jackson, thanks to the summer trade, of late years have become pretty elegant affairs. Not even any sawdust, and there's no use asking what the boys in the back room will have because there no longer are any back rooms, in the fine old American tradition. These now are night clubs or genteel cocktail lounges with soft lights and leather chairs and gleaming roulette wheels or other gambling facilities for the daring, or the rich.

The Silver Dollar Bar, in the Wort Hotel, is a long curved

LOG CABIN CLUB
SILVER DOLLAR BAR
OPEN RANGE
CAFE
CAFE
CAFE
R
J
Bar
BAR
Silver Spur
COCKTAILS
Cowboy BAR
COCKTAILS

bar with 2,032 silver dollars partly embedded in its surface, which is made of an agonizingly tenacious black plastic, evidently invented by the FBI to keep desperate customers out of jail. The rest of the layout, in décor, is on the New York side in approach and intent, which if not quite fully realized in implementation still is darn good and pretty. The Cowboy Bar, large and garish and aimed at the lush summer trade, features a revolving cowboy on its roof and another cowboy lassoing a steer on its façade, all of this in colored neon lights, in full motion. Elegant indeed: an artistic display up to and—some think—far beyond the hilt, frightening the wild geese almost out of their senses.

It took some time for the people of Jackson Hole to take this tourist-engendered posh and glitter in stride. The old Alpine Bar, before the Wort boys apparently held up the Denver mint and went in for culture and peaceful coexistence with the foreigners and turned it into the Silver Dollar, was a favorite with the cowboys. But when it emerged from its chrysalis as a full-fledged butterfly they were leary of it: it looked too much like the kind of place in which you are expected to take off your hat, and any journeyman cowboy would as soon—a hell of a lot sooner, in fact—take off his pants, in any circumstances. (Harry Clissold, Jackson's perpetual mayor and an amateur student of Freud, says that the opposite number of the city feller's nightmare in which he walks up Broadway in the nude is the terrible dream of the cowboy in which he is caught in bed without his hat.)

However, all fears on this vital point were quieted, here and elsewhere around the square, and now the town's four pubs carry on through the cocktail hour in the old-time tradition as the permanent personnel of the Hole, grateful to the summer's paying guests for the mahogany footrests (known in summer as cocktail tables), happily move in after Labor Day, with gusto, for their turn in the parlor.

The first cocktail party I recall ever having attended, anywhere, was in Jackson. This was many years ago, during Prohibition, and the party was held in the United States post office.

It was a bitterly cold December night and I had just arrived in town and was staying at the Crabtree Inn, a small frame structure the rooms of which were unheated in spite of a temperature well into the forty-below zone, and while standing in the small lobby as close to the stove as I could get without contributing to the fire, pensively looking out the window, I saw some cowboys riding past with white bundles tied to the cantles of their saddles. I asked about this and was told that there was a dance in the hall above the drugstore. The white bundles were flour or sugar sacks in which the cowboys had wrapped—never mind the wrinkles—the current Sears, Roebuck version of what the man-about-town wears after dark.

I found that anybody could go to the dance, so, sensing a warmer stove, I dashed over there. I found the stove not only larger but, to my delight, hotter: its great potbelly, trying to digest as much as it could of the surrounding forest, glowed a deep satisfying red. Getting close to it, though, was another matter. The hall was lined with plank benches, and the best ones were taken, but by standing aside until the next dance started I was able to work my way into a comfortable position.

After a while, pressing my luck, I began to wish I had a drink, and right after this I noticed that some of the fellows were going downstairs between dances and showing signs of having had a few.

I saw one of the chaps glancing at me a few times and presently he came over and said, "You look thirsty."

I damned near fell off the bench.

"You are a mind reader," I said.

"Follow me," he said.

My benefactor led me down the stairs, which incidentally were on the outside of the building, past the drugstore and into the adjoining post office, the lobby of which was open all night, the angel of mercy explained. Six or eight others were there, nearly filling the place; they were standing around talking, and taking nips from pint bottles of what I hoped would turn out to be gin. My host went to one of the lockboxes, opened it, withdrew a pint and offered me a drink. It was the finest gin I ever had tasted. We had a few more, and he introduced me around, and we had a pleasant time.

Some of those present had engagements to keep upstairs, so returned their bottles to their mailboxes and left, while others came down to consult their own mailboxes and protect themselves against the weather. My friend had to leave, but I elected to stay and take my chances. My chances turned out well, and I never did go upstairs, returning to my hotel under a paling sky after a final rendition of a musical composition called, I believe, "Sweet Adeline."

I had supposed, of course, that the boys had brought their pints with them for deposit in this exclusive club, but later I came to understand that the government, with an able assist from a large bowl, or tub, in the basement of a nearby church, had consummated the perfect wedding of church and state—the weatherman officiating—in recognition of the spiritual and material facts of life as it must be lived in Jackson Hole, Wyoming, come the blasts of winter across the frozen peaks of the Tetons.

chapter 2

"Care to Step Outside . . . ?"

THE COCKTAIL hour in Jackson Hole is no brawl, either on the verbal side, as when persons try vainly to complete a whole sentence of their own in the crossfire of similar and simultaneous efforts by many others within a restricted area, nor on the physical side, entailing untoward events, as such.

In Jackson the cubic footage personally occupied by each contestant is spacious enough to let you bend your own elbow and drink your own drink and, if you feel like it, scratch your own behind. People even are inclined to spend part of their time talking and part of it listening, an approach that would leave the average New Yorker petrified with horror.

Once Roy Jensen, proprietor of the RJ Bar in Jackson, visited me in New York and I absent-mindedly took him to a cocktail party. Later, after it was over and we had cleared our ears by holding our noses and puffing out our cheeks, we went to a nearby lunch counter and had a chat during which each one of us was allowed to finish a whole paragraph at a time.

"Well, I tell you," Roy shouted, forgetting we had left the party, "the way I see it, everybody and everything here in New York is vertical. People live on a vertical plane, everybody on top of everybody else—excuse the expression —and when it comes to a party they talk and drink and jam up and everybody listens to himself." He looked around and noticed we were nearly alone in the little joint, and lowered his voice to normal. "Take a cocktail party, and you set yourself where your mouth is two inches from somebody's ear, no matter who it is, although the prettier the better, and go to work, and all you care about is the echo. When I tell people around here that our cocktail hour back home lasts a couple of months they seem a little surprised, but it's dollars to doughnuts that if you would take a sound recording of this thing we just came from and sort it out and turn it down so you could hear a few words in a row, on a reasonable basis, it might stretch out, horizontally, for a couple of months at that."

Roy paused, to let me have my say, but I couldn't think of anything . . .

Now we come to that more pointed meaning of the word "brawl," which suggests the occurrence of untoward events. There are a few friendly fights in Jackson Hole during the hour, of course, but nothing, it seems to me, that could be called "untoward." That is to say, nobody gets really mad at anybody else, on anything remotely approaching a permanent basis. It's a sort of local understanding that no matter how hard you accidentally are hit, there's no point in building it up into an unpleasant situation. It's going to be a long, hard winter, with cabin fever just around the corner, and to resent a sock on the nose so early in the season is considered indelicate, or, as the cowboys put it, *de trop*.

The only thing approaching a squabble I ever saw in Jackson Hole was a little rumpus, didn't amount to anything, in the Silver Dollar, in October of either 1950 or 1951. The bar was quite full that night, but there still remained plenty of elbow room. Dennis Morgan, a motion-picture actor, had come up from Hollywood for the hunting season, as per his custom, had got his elk and now was enjoying a libation with his guide, who also was a personal pal.

I had known Morgan for some time and the three of us

got to discussing movie fights, in which no actual blows are struck, both parties cleverly missing but seeming to be getting murdered, the sickening smacks of fist on chin being dubbed in on the sound track later. Morgan offered to show how it was done. He backed up from the bar a couple of feet.

"Swing at me," he told his guide, then quickly added, as an afterthought, "but for Christ sake don't hit me."

The guide swung and Morgan took a beautiful fall, landing on the floor, where he began to twist and turn in an imitation of agony. Then, starting to get up, he said, "See, all we needed was a bottle of ketchup." He turned to me. "Go out to the kitchen and get one, and we'll try it again."

I started in that direction but found my way blocked by a rather unique situation that had developed.

The first thing I remember, vaguely, was being hit on the ear by somebody who, I found later, was aiming a roundhouse right at the guide, who apparently had knocked Morgan, a guest of Jackson Hole, flat on his ass. I knew the blow was not intended for me, personally, because I was wearing glasses, and when anything approaching the untoward happens in Jackson Hole it is gentlemanly through and through.

Morgan—as I recall it—now tried to succor his guide, and to explain matters, but by this time everybody in the Silver Dollar was swinging at everybody else. Nobody knew why. Old friends who had been talking amiably broke off their sentences like so many icicles and bashed each other on the beezer. The floor was covered with corpses, without benefit of ketchup.

Morgan? Who the hell was Morgan? Otherwise gentle cowboys, who wouldn't hurt a fly, and who thought of Morgan, if they thought of him at all, only as a brave Confederate general in the Civil War, swatted their colleagues on the chin.

I don't know where that great American expression, "Do

you care to step outside and repeat that?" came from. What does it mean? The guy has said it, hasn't he? Why does he have to say it again? Why does it have to be outside?

The answers to these questions escape me, but I do know that at a certain point in the festivities now under way this phrase began to be bandied about, and suddenly everybody, at catch weights, whether they were in the main event or the preliminaries, now moved out into the street, leaving the Silver Dollar empty. In no time at all there were six or seven separate groups scattered for more than a block along the street, each one engaged in violent argument, punctuated by occasional physical activity.

Morgan, the forgotten man, now walked up and down the street, from group to group, battlefield to battlefield, patiently explaining what had started it all: just a friendly, private gag. A few tried to take a poke at him, only to discover their error, for this movie actor had, and for all I know still has, as fast a pair of dukes as anybody in Jackson Hole. In the end, he prevailed. A couple of merry-go-rounds disappeared into the night, but most of the soldiers straggled back into the Silver Dollar, picked up their drinks where they had left them, resumed their conversations, and the evening came off as pleasantly and calmly as it had begun, which proves my point. Nothing, it seemed, had happened. Long before dawn the walking wounded, including me with my bad ear, strolled homeward, whistling.

The next day my ear was well, and so was everybody else.*

* My more or less incoherent account of this discussion among friends is substantiated by Jess Wort, co-owner with his brother John of the Silver Dollar. I saw Jess at noon, April 23, 1955, in room 2001, the Savoy-Plaza Hotel, New York City, and mentioned the occurrence. Jess was present at the time and in fact helped Dennis Morgan straighten things out. He had only one thing to add: after everybody had returned to the bar, the house had set up drinks all around. I had missed this, probably because of my bad ear. I now explained this to Jess, stood on my constitutional rights, and he called Room Service and made up for it, and I felt better.

The only other time I personally was injured during that particular cocktail hour in Jackson came about a few weeks later in, of all places, the Elks' Club.

I was struck on the arch of my right foot by a deer head, causing a contusion.

The lodge was putting on a benefit of some kind in behalf of a worthy cause—juvenile delinquency, in fact—and I attended, not only because I was in favor of juvenile delinquency but because the benefit affair was open to all comers, members or not, and the drinks in the Elks' Club were both cheaper and larger than those in the commercial bars. Also attending this function was Slim Linville, the night marshal. This was Slim's evening off and he was enjoying a few drinks, being a little dry and also in favor of the Cause that the lodge was excited about. Behind the bar was Earl Greeno, one of Slim's best friends. Earl had opened a beauty shop in Jackson a few years before but it had perished because nobody cared about it and now, like most other important citizens of the town, he was tending bar. I once knew a chap in Los Angeles who got a job as sweeper-up and handyman in a beauty shop, his name was Bob Burton, before that he had been a barker in a carnival, and the owner of the beauty shop got so far behind in Bob's wages that he finally gave him the keys to the shop and walked off into the eternal night, and Bob did real well.

As Slim was about to leave, a bit after midnight, Earl reminded him that he hadn't settled his account. Slim took some bills from his pocket and was about to pay up when he backed away from the bar and said, in the friendliest possible way, "Maybe you better come and get it."

At the Elks' Club the bartender, as against the practice in lesser saloons, is allowed to take a few snifters of his own, especially during benefits intended to improve the community. Earl had had a couple. In any case he decided to take Slim at his word and hurdled the bar at the point of its junction with the wall. Just above that spot hung a mounted deer head. (The Jackson Elks' Club is the only one in the country that is not adorned with a stuffed elk head, although the largest elk herd in the world lives here.) As Earl cleared the bar he hit this deer head with his shoulder and dislodged it. In falling, one antler point raked Earl's cheek, slightly gashing it. The head caromed over to Slim and the other antler, or maybe the same one, hit him on the chin, cutting it a little.

The deer head then hit your correspondent (me) on the foot, inflicting a painful if not fatal wound, and rolled under the poker table and out of sight.

Each of the stricken men, seeing blood on the other, raised a hand to his own face and, as the saying is, drew color. What the hell! They looked at each other in a kind of dazed amazement. This had happened very quickly, and neither of them, apparently, had seen the deer head, which in any case now was under the poker table. They glanced around to see if some stranger had muscled in, then, finding themselves alone, became locked in combat.

It was not a very good fight, by any standard. Nowadays they have better ones every Friday on television. The technique they used was the one favored by club fighters everywhere: keep swinging, keep missing, keep hoping for the best. How dull can you get? The only person hit with any authority were a couple of friends who tried to intercede, and these quickly backed up out of range, which, the way the boys were flailing away at the air, meant several feet.

Slim, for some reason or other, I couldn't understand why, began backing up and the so-called combat moved out of the bar and onto the dance floor. Where it had belonged in the first place, if you ask me. Slim now made the only mistake I ever had known him to make. He jumped back out of hitting distance, rested a hand on the butt of his revolver, and shouted:

"Earl, you're under arrest!"

Earl dropped his arms, which by this time must have felt like so much soft soap, and thought it over.

"Oh no I'm not," he said. "You're off duty, Slim." With this he stepped in and came up with a roundhouse left that caught Slim flush on the point of the shoulder.

Friends now came to the rescue of both battlers and the carnage was stopped. The thing about the deer head was carefully explained, and all hands returned to the bar for a drink on behalf of the juvenile delinquency thing. Unfortunately, some busybody had fished the deer head out from under the poker table and put it back on the wall. When the gladiators saw this they felt they had been fibbed to and squared off for another round. But the spirit flickered, then died. The wounds were taken care of with the bar towel, and Slim bought a round for the house. I limped around a bit, mentioning that I had been hit on the foot, but nobody seemed impressed.

The friendship of Earl Greeno and Slim Linville carried on as before, but neither one of them, to this day, is taking any nonsense about any roving deer head.

I have mentioned a couple of minor incidents that took place during one of the cocktail hours in Jackson Hole, and that I happened to run across—or, considering my hurt ear and my injured foot, happened to run into. Nothing of a violent nature ever goes on at all. If anybody comes into the Hole looking for real trouble, he can be accommodated, just as he can in Gary, Indiana, but if he expects to see the natives shoot it out among themselves, as a kind of spectator sport, he better go on to the movies and get it out of his system.

Things have not always been so calm in the Hole, to be sure. In the early days there were quite a few misunderstandings that ended in people shooting each other on purpose, or nearly on purpose, give or take a little, but these things had to do with cattle rustling, water rights, highway robbery, murder, and other routine matters. In fact, Jackson Hole at one time had quite a reputation for slightly untoward events —it is the scene of Owen Wister's *The Virginian*—but now the public relations department of the Chamber of Commerce is in charge, pointing out that a fellow could resent being hit by a stray deer head even in New York.

Occasionally motion-picture companies come in to shoot outdoor scenes—*Shane* and *Jubal Troop* were recent ones—and sometimes the tourists, recognizing the background when they get here, seem a little mixed up. One summer evening a plump, broad-beamed visitor, his jowls delicately pinked by the Western sun, draped a Hawaiian-shirted arm over the RJ bar and, after shifting his cigar from one corner of his mouth to the other, without using either hand, asked Jack Francis, giving him a knowing wink, "What time does the shooting start around here, pardner?"

Jack glanced at his wrist watch. "In about twenty, twenty-five minutes," he said.

The foreigner, leaving his unfinished drink on the bar, waddled out into the night, got into his car and dashed away, his tires firing a staccato blast of small pebbles against the window of George Lumley's drugstore.

He hasn't come back, so far.

chapter 3

Shot of Crème de Menthe, Boys?

WHAT would a cocktail hour be without love? Past love to be remembered in moist nostalgia, present love temporarily to be intensified, possible future love to be anticipated, and above and beyond these the most terrifying form of this gentle passion to be met head-on: the lonely unrequited love that lightly sears the soul, leaves a fleeting scar on the impressionable tissue of the heart and a transient tear trembling in the corner of the eye.

To come to the point, when summer ends and winter rears its ugly head, the dude girls go home.

The low moaning wail of the cowboy lies heavy on the land as blood, sweat, and tears combine to form ankle-deep puddles in the sagebrush.*

The lads simply will not learn that "darling" and its tender variations add up to nothing more than conversational semicolons, mere pauses for breath, and that a quick kiss or better down behind the corral is no token of undying love but a quick flip in the hay. No troth is pledged; nobody is engaged to marry nobody. Even when the little lady, entranced by these dramatic surroundings and by an air of romance and his-

* Just as I am using "New York," in this book, in a generic sense, so am I using the term "cowboy" to cover a lot of people. The New Yorker thinks that everybody wearing a large hat and high-heeled boots is a cowboy, although he may be a certified public accountant. By "cowboy" I mean, mostly, cowboys, horse wranglers, dude wranglers, rangers, ranchers, and just about everybody excepting the "Cowboy Trios" in the fancier bars.

tory that she feels are somehow embodied in the cowboy, gets carried away, in body or in spirit, and speaks softly of the Eternal Mountains, she may really mean the mountains, which she can take or leave alone when the chips are down.

Let the older cow hands, their breasts so heavy with scar tissue that they scarcely can take a deep breath, explain to the neophytes that all they're going to get out of it is a picture postcard of the Empire State Building, this makes little impression on the young wise guys, who are sure that this time it's the real thing.

In justice to the dude girl it must be acknowledged that very often she, too, thinks it's the real thing. She may really believe that she is through with the Brooks Brothers suit forever; she is willing to give up all; every cowboy is Hopalong Lochinvar in the living flesh and every tired cayuse is a white steed and she pats both lovingly, her levis limp with sincerity, her eyes shining with high-minded determination. But there is nothing quite so divisive as the Continental Divide, and upon crossing it everything goes to pieces and the post-Labor Day blues come winging in, even for her. Our sweetheart looks backward with red-rimmed eyes until she reaches Omaha, then the horizen swings around in a wide arc and the New York skyline looms high over the prairies with miragelike clarity and behind her she has left a dream, riding . . .

This situation naturally brings up a question: What is the matter with the Western girl, that lovely product of a lovely land, that the cowboys want to bypass her in pursuit of those more fragile dolls?

Bob Crisp, one of the great cowboys of the Hole, once summed it up this way:

"A Western girl is as fine or better than they come, I don't care where it might be, you name it. But still and all these dude girls are pretty good and fancy. No substance, no brains at all, don't know their—you know what I mean. But they have that look of being a nice thing to have around the house, especially on a rainy day. Another thing: when they come out here from where they usually live, off the leash for a while, they are quicker to kiss strangers than the local girls are. This gives them a head start, for a Western girl ninety-nine tenths of the time will not kiss anybody, to say nothing of marrying them, until she knows their name.

"Now take the cowboy. He's just another ranch hand to the local girl, she has saw him a million times and she wishes he would take a bath and brush his teeth. But the dude girl thinks she is in some kind of movie and gets herself mixed up with Mary Pickford, or whoever it is, and gets a lot of ideas, which are more interesting than practical. The way it usually ends, the cowboy is left to cry in his Crème de Menthe, alone, then marry the Western girl, who ninety-nine tenths of the time is better than anything that ever crossed the Mississippi River."

Wait a minute—

Cry into his *what?*

A powerful aromatic manifestation of the lingering culture of the departed dude girl, the only *corpus delicti* you actually can get your teeth into, is a highly visible green drink known as Crème de Menthe.

This is not, if I may venture a bit of understatement, a standard Western drink in the traditional sense. There are two Western drinks, whiskey and beer, and in ordinary times you order either a "drink" or a "beer." You don't have to say what kind of drink: a drink is a drink. The new potion is called, with some diffidence—a person doesn't like to show off his French in public—a "green," or "a green one." So you now can order a drink, a beer, or a green one. This

Johnny-come-lately looks very much like a spray, either for potato plants or for the nasal passage, but it easily can be taken orally, especially if the tear ducts already are clogged, which they usually are. The dude girls liked it frappéd last summer, but the cowboys and other mourners during the cocktail hour take it straight or mixed with water, with a slice of nostalgia on the rim of the glass—which, after being emptied, often is hurled into a corner of the barroom and smashed to bits, after the old Air Force ritual.

Ordering a drink of this poisonous-looking fluid is something of a ritual in itself. The first thing you do upon coming up to the bar is to wipe your eyes with the sleeves of your windbreaker, or winter underwear, or whatever you have on, so you can manage to find the concoction after it's served. You then place both elbows carefully upon the bar and use your hands to cup the chin, which ought to be trembling a little. Look straight ahead into the backbar mirror. When the bartender comes up to you, don't pay any attention to him. Whisper to yourself (in the mirror), "A green one, Steve."

Steve nods sympathetically, or, if you're not looking at him, grunts sympathetically. He murmurs, "I know just what you mean, Slim. I been through it a couple times myself. Take it easy, boy. Single one, or double?"

(Steve, who also is a salesman, has you there. Maybe all you want is a single one, but you can't let the little lady down. A gentleman orders double.)

Today the green one accounts for roughly one-sixth of Jackson bar sales during the cocktail hour. The graph then slips sideways and downhill but the demand continues all winter on this diminishing scale, sluffing off sharply in the spring as the *blessés* readjust themselves to the American way of life and hope sings anew through the cracks and crevices of the heart and all eyes turn toward the Continental Divide, confidence rampant that the new crop may be even better than that of last year . . .

It is only natural that this consumption of Crème de Menthe should be subject to abuses and subversive adaptation. A certain number of romantic racketeers who never have been within a hundred yards of a dude girl in their lives go through the green-one routine in the same spirit that prompts a hopelessly homely babe to buy her own engagement ring. It is an inexpensive but often effective exercise in bootstrap-lifting, and many a young fellow hitherto unappreciated by the local distaff finds himself suddenly looked at with pointed interest, a rather gay chap, after all, hard to get, an eligible bachelor, as the saying goes, just because he can lift a glass of Crème de Menthe to the eye level and look through it with a vague expression.

This also has proved of value to many a rheumatic Lothario, his days of dalliance long past, by this simple expedient approximating the Fountain of Youth in synthetic kudos, wearing the dishonorable but always intriguing badge of the man who has kissed, and told.

I would not be projecting the whole truth, though, were I to suggest that the dude girl-cowboy impact never came to anything other than disappointment, frustration, despair, and the green bottle. There have been a number of happy results, testified to by the fact that many of the children in Jackson Hole today are halfbreeds.

One summer a conducted tour from the East, made up of forty persons, mostly assorted schoolteachers, arrived at the little settlement of Moran (Pop. 21) at the northern tip of the Hole thirty-three miles from Jackson. They were headed for Yellowstone Park. It was one of those things where the clients pay one-half the cost of the excursion at the start and the balance when they get to the halfway point, which in this case happened to be Moran.

The curriculum included a week-long pack trip into the mountains from Lester Leek's dude ranch at nearby Turpin Meadow. The impresario, whose name was Jackson, saw them off for the hills, waved an enthusiastic goodby, returned to his car, gunned the engine, and never has been seen since, by anybody concerned. Since this was an all-expense tour, the happy vacationists upon returning from the pack trip found themselves flat of pocket. Lester Leek was left holding his share of the bag but put the strandees up until they could get money to take them back home.

Word flew around the Hole with the approximate speed of nuclear fission, and with roughly the same impact, that Turpin Meadow was loaded to the gills with impounded schoolteachers and other choice items. This news touched off a headlong rush such as the Tetons never had seen before and are not likely to see again, barring the discovery of uranium.

The main idea was to get there first, or as near first as possible, because all schoolteachers do not look alike and if you're late all the best ones may be spoken for. The theory here is that if you have a car you are three jumps ahead of the contestant who does not have a car but has a horse, and at least fifty jumps ahead of the one who has nothing but a pair of boots.

But variable factors enter. An automobile has to follow the road, which may not in all cases happen to be the shortest distance between two points, thus a good cowboy on a good horse, sometimes a medium cowboy on a medium horse, often can take enough short cuts to get there ahead of the car. There is much to be said, too, for the man on foot. Right at the start he does not have to corral a horse or warm up an engine: he can just start running. He may beat the horse.

He can dash through a dense stand of lodgepole pine that a horse would have to go around, and he can ford streams faster than a horse can, supposing the horse never to have seen a beautiful schoolteacher in his life.

The race to Turpin Meadow was a memorable one.

A sudden mountain downpour added drama by swelling the streams and muddying-up the dirt roads. Let one car bog down, and no others could pass. There was one good gravel road leading into Moran from the south (Jackson Hole) side, one coming down from Yellowstone Park, to the north, while a third came in from the east over the Continental Divide through Togwotee Pass. Although Turpin Meadow was on this last road, the one over which the tour had come in to the Hole, the nearest town, Dubois, was ninety miles away and was not considered a serious threat with respect to anybody this side of General Sheridan. The road from Yellowstone was another matter. This was the best one of all, and although the distance from Park Headquarters to Moran, or Turpin Meadow, was greater than that from Jackson, the excellent condition of the road was a disturbing factor.

Even more distressing than this—it having been assumed that the Turpin Meadow news had reached the Park—was the fact that the Park Rangers wore uniforms. This was before the cowboys had become conscious of the sartorial effectiveness of their own work clothes, and they looked at the forest-green uniforms and stiff-brimmed Stetsons of the rangers as being sheer murder.

Before telling you who won, I should like to point out certain facts of life. A man in an automobile, having read the various advertisements, is inclined to think, even when he is bogged down, that he is jet-propelled, and he has a tendency to count his schoolteachers before they are hatched. A horse has to be fed, and on top of this does not like to travel at night, especially when taking short cuts over rough terrain. The Turpin Meadow news had reached Jackson, and spread through the Hole, late in the afternoon—a Wednesday, if memory serves.

Now we come to the infantry. The foot soldier, to start with, has an inferiority complex. He knows he is not jet-propelled, his feet hurt, he is ready to concede victory, in any race, before he starts. But he has two things on his side: he has an indomitable will and he can travel all night without stopping.

This last consideration, undoubtedly, was the decisive one.

A limping, wet, muddy, exhausted Jackson Holer staggered into the camp at Turpin Meadow just as the stranded tourists were lining up for breakfast. He looked them over, twice, then decided to try for the jackpot. He hobbled up to the prettiest one in sight, bowed, said "Hello, sucker," and collapsed. He couldn't lose, after that: he had himself a lovely wife.*

Other Jackson Hole troopers arrived soon thereafter, followed by the Yellowstone Park drum majors, but the Hole contingent, in a rare show of community spirit, put on an impromptu rodeo the next day and this settled the hash of the outsiders and many friendships were established, a few of them ripening into love, if I may borrow an expression from Miss Dorothy Dix, and, in marriage ties, contributing both to the population and the general well-being of this mountain valley.

In any case the Turpin Meadow stampede is thought of as having been a turning point in the social and cultural

* This was Esther Bulwan, daughter of Mr. and Mrs. C. A. Bulwan of 4512 Tonawanda Drive, Des Moines, Iowa. A graduate of Drake University, she was teaching school at Salix, Iowa. As Esther Allan, wife of Karl (Sunny) Allan, now a Grand Teton National Park ranger, she is one of the foremost personalities, and decorations, of Jackson Hole. I always am delighted when invited to their charming log-cabin home, for I love them both, and on top of this Esther makes the best sourdough pancakes I ever have known.

history of the community. A number of dude girls since have joined the permanent personnel and every one of them has turned out fine and dandy. Not only on rainy days, but all the time.

Now we come to another subject, or rather to another phase, or angle, of the same subject. This has to do with the cowboys who, upon receiving a picture postcard of the Empire State Building with "Wish you were here" scrawled across it, take it literally, not as a casual social amenity but as something in the nature of a summons, verging on breach of promise, a challege to one's honor. The cowboy, by and large, is a conscientious fellow; he wants to do what is expected of him, for he is imbued with the traditional Western approach to what used to be called the sanctity of womanhood. I don't know what it is called now.

More than one, upon being served with this document, has put his summer's wages into a suit of clothes, a white shirt, a shave, haircut and railroad ticket, and has traveled to New York (San Francisco, New Orleans, Philadelphia, Memphis, Cleveland, Des Moines, Minneapolis, Chicago, Key West) either to carry out what he looked at as his obligation or, in some cases, simply to press his luck.

I have very little good news here, although once a cowboy friend of mine made one of the most brilliant pitches I ever heard of in my life. He arrived, unannounced, in New York City and at the Park Avenue apartment in which his supposed baby lived. Obviously puzzled, perhaps fooled by his suit of clothes, she finally remembered who he was and received him cordially, introducing him to her parents, and, after dinner, to her fiancé.

Coincidentally, the rodeo just then was on at Madison Square Garden. Our cowboy, accepting his defeat with becoming grace, offered to get the girl and her beau a couple of box seats for the next night—a thing he easily could do, because his old friend Tex Austin, for whom he had worked several times as a performer, was running the show.

The New Yorkers were pleased to accept, and the cowboy got the tickets from Tex. Then he came up with an idea. He had met the girl in Jackson Hole during a rodeo in which he was an outstanding contestant, a circumstance that in fact had led to their brief romance. Having nothing to lose and everything to gain, he now got Austin to put him on as a substitute rider in the saddle-bronc event, borrowed some gear, and made a terrific ride in front of his guests, duplicating what the lady had seen him do in the larger arena of Jackson Hole.

This inspired strategy came within an eyelash of working. I'm sorry it didn't, not only for his sake, but, selfishly enough, for my own, because if it had panned out I would have a much better story to tell. Limited here to the truth, all I can say is that he returned to Jackson Hole, alone, putting away one Crème de Menthe after another in the club car of the train.

chapter 4

The Dodgers Win the Fourth Game

EVER since the radio manufacturers began to make sets that were efficient enough to overcome the static and other technical obstacles set up by the Tetons—and there was nothing easy about this—the World Series has taken on a fresh importance here in the Hole. It always has been a high point of the cocktail hour, followed through newspaper accounts and by quick surreptitious phone calls to Idaho Falls or Salt Lake City by persons who want to lay down a bet on the game just as soon as they know who has won it. But now that science at long last had beaten the metal-and-granite barriers that surround the valley and culture is pouring in like Niagara Falls the Series has reached in impact a level not too far removed from that of life and death itself.

This comes natural to an area in which partisanship, for its own sake, is an integral part of ordinary existence: everything automatically becomes an Issue, and whether anybody understands what it's all about is beside the point. The main thing is to choose up sides first and ask questions later, if at all. In the matter of the World Series, there are no neutrals, even among those who think baseball is a game played with a deck of cards, the joker and the one-eyed jacks wild, or has something to do with horseshoes. The division between the

Dodger people (Democrats) and the higher-class rooters for the Yankees (Republicans) is so acute that during the Series all friendships are suspended. More marksmen can be seen practicing on the shooting range on Bill Fleishmann's ranch just before the Series than at any other time of the year.

The foremost Dodger fan extant, certainly the most isolated and remote one, so far as I have been able to find out, is a resident of the Hole. His name is Frenchy (no middle initial) and he traps for a living far up the Buffalo Fork, a major local tributary of the Snake River, just under the Continental Divide. Frenchy comes to Jackson twice a year, once in the spring to ship out his pelts, once in the fall to buy his supplies for the winter.

Mayor Harry Clissold told me about Frenchy, not as a Dodger fan but as a trapper, a so-called "character," and an individual. He suggested that were I to get together with Frenchy, and by some hocus-pocus get him to talking, I might find out his life story, whatever it was, and in any case get his philosophy of life—all persons who live in remote cabins are philosophers to end all philosophers, if you can get them to talking—and come up with a book. Harry offered to act as a mutual friend, the next time Frenchy came to town.

So one day Harry looked me up and told me, not without excitement, that Frenchy was in, and at that very minute was at the Silver Dollar. Here, Harry said, was my chance. I was not too enthusiastic about my "chance," for I had met a million or so Frenchies, always at the insistence of persons who thought I ought to write a book and wanted to help. But I appreciated Harry's kindness, and we went over there.

"Buy him a drink right away," Harry said as we approached the saloon, "and give Willard Miner the high sign to keep his glass filled. If he's in the mood, he'll start talking, and if he once starts talking you've got your book."

Frenchy turned out to be an elderly gentleman with a marked resemblance to Marshal Pétain. Upon our being introduced by His Honor he glanced at me and nodded casually. Harry ordered drinks from Willard, tossed his off quickly, then after giving me an encouraging wink across Frenchy's back discreetly withdrew.

"So you're from New York," Frenchy said. "Live anywhere near Brooklyn?"

"Just across the river," I said.

Frenchy looked at me with something approaching interest. "Ever hear of a baseball team called the Dodgers?" he asked.

"I've seen them play many times," I said. "I'm what is known as a Dodger fan."

Frenchy turned to Willard and gave him the nod. "Another drink for Mr. . . . ah . . . for the gentleman," he said. He looked at me with a show of enthusiasm. "Well, well, *well!* You're just the man I want to see. Please tell me, why did Dressen yank Newcombe and bring in Branca to throw that home-run ball to Bobby Thomson and lose the Giant playoff for the pennant? Have you got the lowdown on that one?"

Willard gave me my drink. "It wasn't a home-run ball," I said, "except that Bobby hit it for one. I mean, it wasn't a cripple. It was high and inside and he powdered it. He's a good batter."

"He's a lousy batter," Frenchy said. He looked at me suspiciously. "You don't seem to care that he hit it out of the park. You seem God damn calm about it, if you ask me. You sound more like a Giant fan than a Dodger fan." He glanced at my drink, and I had a feeling he was going to ask Willard to take it back and refund his money.

"See here," I said, finishing my drink to be sure I had it, "I'm just telling you how it was. It couldn't be helped. Branca says he'd pitch the same ball again, and so does Campanella. Campanella would have called for the same pitch from Newcombe, if he had stayed in."

"How do you know that?" Frenchy demanded.

"Branca and Campanella both told me," I said.*

Frenchy appeared stunned. "My God!" he said. "Do you mean you know the Dodgers in person?"

"Not all of them," I said.

Frenchy looked at my glass and saw that it was empty. "Willard!" he called. "What goes on around here? Can't you see that this fellow's glass is empty? Why," he asked me, "is Hodges such a sucker for the low outside curve?"

"He's not a sucker for it," I explained. "That's just a fable, one that Hodges may have set up himself. It's a hard pitch to throw, just at the edge of the plate, and Hodges gets more balls than strikes on it. It's not uncommon for a big-league player, especially a good one like Hodges, to miss a certain kind of pitch by about two feet, now and then, just to get the pitcher to keep throwing it."

"I'll be a son of a bitch," Frenchy said thoughtfully.

"How is everything in the trapping business?" I asked. "Are fur prices holding up?"

"Oh, the hell with it!" Frenchy said. He looked up the bar. "Willard! Are you paralyzed, or what?"

"It's my turn to buy," I said.

"The pleasure is mine," Frenchy said. "Now tell me, when Bill Bevens had a no-hitter, and Cookie Lavagetto came to bat in the ninth inning . . . "

* Although this is true in fact, it is not true in context. I did not discuss this with Campanella and Branca until some time after I had seen Frenchy. The trapper and I talked about the play, and about the Dodgers, until I was done in. I did not say this to Frenchy. The dialogue here is an accurate reflection of our discussion, if not perfect in detail.

Two hours later I saw Harry Clissold in the RJ Bar. He asked me if I had been talking with Frenchy all this time and I said that I had, and he was delighted.

"I've never known Frenchy to talk that long," he said. "Did you get his whole story? Did you get a lot of stuff?"

"I think so," I said in a hoarse voice. "By the way, Frenchy is something of a baseball fan."

Harry shrugged. "A peculiarity of his," he said. "A friend of his at the Moran post office saves all the sports sections of the Denver *Post* and takes them up to Frenchy a couple of times during the summer. Then he puts them in order, by date, and reads one each day. He's in favor of the Dodgers, but you can't hold that against Frenchy. He means well. He has lived an interesting life, hasn't he? I hope you got enough for a book."

I closed my eyes . . .

"One thing about it," Frenchy is telling his pal at Moran, on his way to his cabin with his supplies for the winter, "every time you go into Jackson you meet an interesting character. Ran across an old gent from New York this trip. Knows all the Dodger players by their first names. Used to pitch for the old Baltimore Orioles, himself, under John McGraw. Hard to get him started talking, but you just buy him a few drinks, keep his glass filled . . . Why, a fellow could write a book . . . When Branca pitched that home-run ball to Bobby Thomson, Roy Campanella . . ."

I opened my eyes and looked at Harry. "Perhaps not enough for a whole book," I said, "but maybe something I could put *into* a book."

Harry nodded. "I see," he said. "Good."

The mayor of Jackson had done his best.

The only time I heard the World Series over the radio in Jackson was the year Willard Miner bought his wonderful portable set. This had cost him $140 at Idaho Falls and not only was far and away the finest outfit in the Hole but the best that money could buy anywhere. He was at great pains to get it in over Teton Pass in time for the Series.

It was only natural for Willard to be the one to have this fine portable radio. He was a man of many hobbies. For example, he had a collection of just under one hundred mechanical pencils, or whatever they are called. Each one was different, either in basic structure or in the advertising imprint on it, if it had an advertising imprint. Nearly a hundred of these is quite a few. Willard had them neatly wired to a large display board in his cabin.

He also was widely known as the foremost exponent, and practitioner, of the old-fashioned waltz not only in Jackson Hole but throughout the Intermountain West, as far south as the Denver-Salt Lake City line. He had won twenty-three out of twenty-four first prizes in the annual contest at the Old Timers' Ball in Jackson, and once was runner-up for the championship of Colorado, just missing. He was a perpetual winner of the Wyoming championship, of course. (I often have thought that if Willard had gone in for boxing he would have held the heavyweight championship longer than anybody else. He had the build, the bone structure, even the features, of the born fighter. I have seen worse waltzers than Willard wear the championship belt.)

He also had the best jackknife in town.

The only fault that anybody could find with Willard, personally, was his curious, unreasoning, almost demoniacal devotion to the New York Yankees. This was quite upsetting to Mr. Dews, a man of years and dignity who kept the Silver Dollar Bar swamped out and lived in the basement beneath it. There he had a corner space, or apartment, two walls of which were formed by stacks of beer cases reaching almost to the ceiling.*

As Frenchy did, Mr. Dews enthusiastically favored the Dodgers. He worked until late at night, or rather until early in the morning, as his duties demanded, and as a consequence seldom rose until well toward noon. During the regular baseball season whenever Willard got news, through the papers that came in with the mail, that the Yankees had won a ball game, it was his custom to strike the floor of the barroom, which also was the ceiling of the apartment of Mr. Dews, three times, heavily, with the sawed-off baseball bat that he kept on hand for packing ice around the beer coils, and for emergency use. (I do not intend here to draw any sociological parallel between the physical juxtaposition of Willard and Mr. Dews and the economic status of Yankee versus Dodger fans; I am just reporting the facts.)

However, to get back to Willard's radio.

He tried it out in his cabin and it worked beautifully, but when he took it over to the Silver Dollar for the Series and set it up on the backbar where he could listen to it, besides entertaining the customers at the bar, it was a sickening disappointment. The Silver Dollar is encased within the heavy masonry and structural steel elements of the Wort Hotel. This probably accounted for the difference. However, the radio for some reason or other worked quite well in the adjoining cocktail lounge, which now was closed for the season, but it wasn't loud enough to be heard in the bar, which clearly left Willard out of it.

* This arrangement may sound dull, but it had its advantages, some of which I shall later explore. One of them was that the beer cases, made of cardboard, easily could be slit with a good sharp knife. By handling this situation judiciously, with a sense of structural stress and strain, Mr. Dews was able to enjoy many a drink on the house, even to entertain an occasional guest. He favored the lower cartons, which, since he was in charge of stacking the beer, he knew wouldn't be reached for some years.

He set it up in the lounge, however, and invited one and all to go in and listen. He felt he could spend some time in there himself. But to his dismay, and his nonconcealed anger, the bar kept him busy, and he was able to find only an occasional minute to sneak into the lounge and ask questions.

"What's the score?" he would ask. "Who's pitching? What inning is it? Anybody on base? Who's up at bat?"

If it happened to be between innings, he usually got a few snatches of information, but if things were tense, just when he most wanted to know what was going on, all he got was "Shhhhhhhhh! Get away! We're trying to listen to this ball game!"

Willard gradually got discouraged about the whole thing, and during the late innings of the fourth game he lost his temper. He had dropped a bet to Mr. Dews and was trying to make a comeback. The score was close, he had a bit of money as well as his heart riding the line, and he was sweating. Some hunters were in, from New York; they didn't give a damn about the World Series, all they wanted was an elk, and Willard was busy, moving up and down behind the bar at a fast trot, when loud exclamations came from the lounge.

He dashed in there.

"What is it?" he demanded. "Who did it? What's the score? Was it a home run? Who's pitch——"

"Shhhhhhhhh! Shhhhhhhh!" everybody said.

Willard marched to the radio and turned it off. "I can go without hearing the score just as long as any son of a bitch in this room can," he said bitterly. He picked up the radio, and started to walk out with it.

The objections were immediate, violent, and began to verge on the physical. Willard stopped. "Wait a minute," he said. "This is my radio. I got it in from Idaho Falls so I could listen to the Series. I'll leave it here, provided I get a report, at the bar, on every batter, every hit, and every everything else, no matter what it is. Otherwise, off she goes, and I don't mean maybe."

He sat pretty after that. The men in the lounge set up a kind of messenger service that brought him not only hits, putouts, and runs, but even individual balls and strikes.

The Dodgers won and Willard got mad all over again. "They wouldn't even let me listen to my own radio," he said, "and the sonabitching Dodgers take the game."

"The Dodgers might have won anyway," I suggested.

Willard shrugged; he wasn't so sure about that.

"Another thing," I said, "the fellows didn't know it was your radio until you told them. You forgot to mention it to start with. They were terribly sorry after they found out about it. So they tried to make it up to you, the best way they could. Also," I added, lying in my own teeth, "most of them were Yankee fans."

Willard rolled a cigarette and lit it, and grinned.

"That makes me feel a lot better about it," he said.

chapter 5

The Office Party

SOON after Labor Day, following the flight of the dudes and the tourists, the extra indoor workers who had come in last June for the lush summer season begin to go away. A few stay on for the relatively minor afterglow of the hunting season but most of them are gone by mid-October, or before, moving out in concert with the yellowing of the quaking-aspen leaves, fluttering away from a dying market to others that just now are approaching seasonal peaks in Nevada, Arizona, California, and similar winter pastures.

These are the male and female shills, the cocktail waitresses and restaurant workers, the gamblers, dealers, bartenders, singing "cowboy" guitar strummers, and other specialists—some of them pretty acute specialists. Many of them come into the Hole year after year, a few buy homes (they sure as hell can afford it) and become legal residents, casting their vote for the superintendent of schools before pulling out for Las Vegas. During this period the air is full of farewells as friends and colleagues part for the winter, to meet again, perhaps, come Memorial Day.

In September, 1950, a bartender by the name of Jack Banning, a friend of mine, who for several seasons had watched these goodbys dribbling along without form or pattern—he was a commuter from points in the Southwest himself—came up with a thought. Why not have a Jackson Hole version of the office party, a national institution beginning to rival the cocktail hour itself in importance, the same as in New York: a gathering of persons united in a shared experience, engaged in the same general line of endeavor, in a climactic affair with some plan and substance to it?

The idea itself caught on at once, although there were some differences of opinion as to its implementation. Two opposing groups quickly emerged. Jack suggested a picnic, an outdoor excursion into the nearby lovely hills—a radical change in scene—but strong opposition developed. Many felt that the party ought to be held in familiar surroundings, the kind they all were used to and in which they would feel more at home. In one of the bars, perhaps, on a Sunday or after closing. Why go out and face the possibility of sunburn, or if not sunburn almost surely rain, with an outside chance, God help everybody, of an early skift of snow? Many other dangers loomed. If not ants, then coyotes.

How about those coyotes?

They already were howling in the hills as they moved slowly into the lowlands, following the game animals to winter quarters, and they sounded hungry. Was there any assurance that a coyote knew the difference between a baby elk and a baby white girl?

An impasse developed, but just in the nick of time, with the days slipping away, some genius came up with a compromise so startlingly simple, so constructive in approach, that all the others wished they had thought of it first.

Most of the female shills and cocktail waitresses, a couple of entertainers and some ladies temporarily at liberty, lived together in a large house, the home of Pat Patterson, a veteran poker-table houseman and free-lance gambler. Pat's place had some eight or nine rooms, plus a small attic dormitory and several improvised rooms in the basement. It was quite an establishment. The girls shared the kitchen, made up their own rules of conduct—which were rigid, don't get Pat wrong and don't get me wrong—and otherwise ran their sorority.

The man who had the constructive idea—can't remember who it was; could have been me, for all I know—suggested that here was a great big house, one of the largest in town, away from sunburn, rain, snow, ants, blisters, and, especially, coyotes. In the back yard was a croquet layout, one large tree and two smaller ones, and a view of the mountains. Here the office party could be held both indoors and out, pleasing everybody, all at the same time.

The impact of this proposal was terrific; even the most blowed-in-the-bottle protagonists of the picnic were back on their heels, stunned.

It was a winner, but only up to a point. Second thoughts came into it, and complications, some of them marital in nature, began to emerge. The whole structure collapsed, sickeningly, when Pat Patterson got wind of it. He slammed his foot down so hard that the Tetons themselves trembled. While expressing full confidence in the decorum of his tenants, he nevertheless pointed out that *this* house was a home, and there would be no unfounded gossip. He never had seen an office party in his life, but he had read about them. No soap.

The Banning forces now came through with what turned out to be the conclusive argument for the picnic. Why, they asked the others, did the dudes come all the way from New York, or wherever the hell they originated, at enormous expense, to enjoy the things that lay right in the office party's lap, free of charge? Surely so many foreigners couldn't be wrong. There must be something to this thing. And then the clincher: Who do these dudes think they are, do they have a mortgage on the country, do they consider themselves better than other people?

Everybody now began to get sore at the dudes, the hell with them, and the picnic carried by acclamation, evidently to put the dudes in their place.

The rest was routine. Time: the following Sunday, beginning early in the morning so the night people could go directly from work, and so a full day in the wilderness could be enjoyed. As many as possible were to wear cowboy clothes or accessories, and transportation was to be by both horse and automobile, according to choice. Horsemen to start at sunup, motorists two hours later. The rendezvous: a grassy, parklike bench, flanked by a pretty grove of quaking aspen and lodgepole pine, on Flat Creek, where it comes out of the hills, six miles from the metropolitan center.

Next came the work of a committee—Jack Banning, chairman—the duty of which was to put the bee on the bars, but plenty, in the matter of refreshments, and on the restaurants, for grub. This operation was more or less scientific, no guessing, no argument, just hand them a list. Joe Madden, one of the Hole's foremost horse wranglers, a man aware of the side upon which his oats were buttered, quickly came through with fourteen saddle horses and two mules.

So the great day approached.

All hands watched the weather with interest and anticipation, about half of them hoping it would turn out to be the finest day of the year and the other half, who began to feel they had been stampeded by this dude thing, their old fears again rampant, praying with might and main for the worst storm ever to sweep the whole Intermountain West so the party would be forced indoors, perhaps to one of the cocktail lounges, there to enjoy central heating and other manifestations of the life civilized.

The Sunday morning, to the mixture of delight and dismay that I have indicated, fortunately or unfortunately dawned with thunderous calm and quiet o'er the Divide: sky clear, a

few zephyrs gently wafted, light mists floating like thin skeins of delicate gossamer among the hills, the snow on the great peaks of the Tetons glowing pink in anticipation of the sun's journey through still one more glorious autumn day in Jackson Hole.

Those who started by horse, although blinking a little in the unfamiliar brightness, looking askance at the sun, a phenomenon of nature that some of them perhaps had not seen for a couple of years, made quite an impressive group, especially when the horses were standing still. As agreed, all wore cowboy regalia, in whole or in token, and the ladies, who had not been hired for their various jobs because they knew how to bake bread, were extremely, in some cases excruciatingly, pretty.

The troupe left town in a small compact formation, a few even attempting a jolly little song, but not all of these cavaliers arrived at Flat Creek at the same time, or on the same horse, if any. A hard determined core of the adventurers made it all the way in the saddle, to be sure, but long before the halfway point was reached others were walking, or trying to walk, either with their horses or to hell with the horses, while some of the more seriously wounded were sitting beside the trail waiting to be picked up by the Cadillacs.

In time most of them got to the beautiful grotto in which the office party was to be held, but right at first there were some mighty anxious moments. The joint having been cased, rests having been taken, somebody made a distressing discovery: Jack Banning was missing.

Where was Jack Banning, with the food and liquor, especially the liquor?

Consternation now rode a fiery steed.

The sun by this time was well up over the nearest hills and splashing itself over the majestic peaks across the valley: the granite now was a glowing lavender, the snow and the glaciers an entrancing gold, and even the upper pine forests were washed, once over lightly, with the same pastel cast. The grove at hand caught a few transient beams, enhancing the yellow of the quaking aspen. Flat Creek gurgled past in dainty post-summer song as wild Canada geese, white chin-straps gleaming, honked their way over the meadows, headed for breakfast.

But where is Jack Banning with that God damn liquor?

The ladies, already up past their bedtime, put on dark glasses against the unaccustomed glare of a light that nobody had turned on, and some of the blackjack dealers got out their eyeshades, perhaps wondering if the magic tints would work outdoors as well as in as they pulled them down along their noses and looked through them.

As thirst and hunger stalked the land in apocalyptic fury, the more imaginative of the distaff element began to hear the cry of the wild wolves in the uplands, perhaps closing in for the kill, and a rumor that those large birds flying past, honking like that, were in fact vultures swept the grove.

"I could eat a horse," a shill said.

She was deluged with offers.

"I knew something like this would happen," a bartender said quietly, "if I would come up to this sonabitching country without my snowshoes."

The pioneers now held a council, and a dash back to the settlements was discussed, but just then some scouts who had ventured down the back trail to look for Indians sent up a faint cheer, and this was picked up by sentinals who had been posted against the coyotes, and word was passed from soldier to soldier:

A small cloud of dust was seen down the road!

Banning!

But cool heads cautioned against undue optimism. Keep

your powder dry, boys! It may be succor, again it may be a sneak attack. Grim-lipped, the doughty garrison—first herding the womenfolk into the Alamo stockade, where they began tearing up their lingerie for bandages—stared down the road. The column of dust grew taller . . . it came closer . . . closer . . . and suddenly a dark object was discernible at its base.

A cry of joy went up as it emerged in clear outline and the tires were seen to be whitewalls, and the body by Fleetwood. The top was down and in the bow stood a heroic figure of a man, the tail of his coonskin cap whipping madly in the Cadillac-engendered breeze.

"Davy Crockett!" the garrison cried as one woman.

The great car drew up with a flourish and very, very eager hands reached out to help unload the ammunition as Davy explained that they had been delayed because of one of those horrors of the General Motors frontier, a dry universal joint.

So the office party, no longer a dry joint of any kind (excuse me; I couldn't help that one), was on at last.

Was it a success?

Does Macy's tell Gimbel's?

Yes, Virginia, it was a success.

It is late afternoon. The sun has crossed the heavens still once more and apparently is about to be speared by the topmost spike of the Grand Teton. A lone cowboy is walking slowly down the bed of a small rocky stream, leading his faithful horse—or a lone horse is walking slowly down the bed of a small rocky stream, pushing his faithful cowboy ahead of him; have it your own way, it makes no difference.

The poor cowboy is tired. Now and then he stops and sits down on a rock, either accidentally or on purpose, takes off his cowboy boots and pours the water from them, slowly, thoughtfully, with his eyes closed. He lets the clear cold water of the stream run over his swollen feet for a few minutes, then pulls the boots back on, which is no child's play, gets up and wearily stumbles on, for he is indomitable.

The horse is patient, in a gentle, sneering, belligerent sort of way, about the whole thing. He knows he is going to be late for supper, he is sure his wife will not believe such an unlikely tale about a cowboy, but if he only knew that his floundering companion of the stream was wearing, or trying to wear, the first pair of cowboy boots he ever had had on, and that the horse himself was the first horse he ever had ridden, or tried to ride, in his whole life, he might have found room for a touch of compassion.

Perhaps the cowboy has had a bit of something to drink, but for a professional dealer of roulette he has an amazing understanding of nature. He knows that water runs downhill, unlike whiskey, which runs uphill, and that if he keeps on following this stream he anyway is sure as hell not going back into the mountains, which are full of coyotes.

The poor cowboy not only is tired, he is lost.

If he were not lost he would kick the horse in the slats and send him away, the farther the better, and go on home alone. But, although he knows he is going downhill, he does not know which hill it is. That is where the horse comes in. As soon as they come to level ground, it will be up to the horse to find the town of Jackson, because the horse lives in Jackson, and the cowboy has read someplace or other that once you get a horse on level ground he knows where he is at.

But why isn't the cowboy riding the horse right now, instead of floundering around among the boulders? Because he has tried it, and has found that you fall harder, and it hurts more, if you begin the fall from the back of a huge horse than if you are closer to the ground, or whatever it is you are falling onto, or into, to start with. Also, the cowboy is taking most of the punishment with his feet, whereas while on the horse he was being murdered all over, or nearly all over.

So, tossed on the horns of a whole herd of yearling dilemmas, he struggles on into the sunset, or what he thinks is the sunset—it could be tomorrow's sunrise—hoping for the best.

He has one consolation: of the sixteen riders—fourteen on horses, two on mules—who started out from Jackson that morning, he is the only one who had the guts to try to get back the same way . . .

At about this time, a string of automobiles can be seen entering the town of Jackson. They are full of people, or what used to be people in the good old days of that morning. Even in the fading light it is plain that the cheeks of the female corpses, which were pink to start with, now not only are much pinker but that this dangerous inflammation has spread over the entire face, excepting only disklike areas around the eyes, which have been protected by sunglasses and remain white, giving them an oddly night-owlish appearance.

Are these by any chance a bunch of rich dudes who have come out from New York to see the wonders of Jackson Hole, to enjoy this lovely and dramatic country to the hilt, and as nature-lovers to stand in awe before the majestic spectacle of the Tetons?

Alas, they are not. They are just some ordinary people, even as you and I are, who have had an office party: just some indoor-lovers trying to get back indoors, where mankind lives in the raw, away from the artificial values of an artificial way of life.

So back to the warmth and comfort and protection of the

only womb they know, unbitten by coyotes, unscalped by Indians, the tired pioneers (one of whom was said to have planted an American flag on Flat Creek) are ready for a night of sweet repose and horrible dreams. Tomorrow they will be back on the job: the gambler to manipulate his cards and his dice and his ivory ball, the cocktail waitress graciously to serve a tinkling glass, the bartender deftly to twirl his tall spoon, the cook, at long last, mission accomplished, returning to the only range he knows anything about, the one in his beloved kitchen.

Part 2. COME AND GET IT!

chapter 6

Some Other Guests

SO THE coyotes lost out on the office party deal as the cocktail waitresses and the beautiful shills, juicy and tender as so many corn-fed heifers, took evasive action and were able successfully to return to the hunting grounds of wolves much larger than any coyote and capable, perhaps, of better-laid plans. The coyote, to be truthful about it, is a rather jolly companion, in a pinch, nothing at all like the snarling beast the old U.S. Biological Survey pictured when, armed to the teeth with mimeograph machines, it set out to rid the ranges both of this highly publicized little animal and of any voters who were opposed to larger Congressional appropriations for this worthy agency.

This was a long time ago. When it was discovered that the coyotes really were public benefactors—picking up a crippled lamb or calf now and then, to be sure, or an occasional cocktail waitress, but mostly living off rodents that did vast damage to the range at the grass roots—one of our most wily and intelligent wild creatures may have been saved from extinction.

Jackson Hole, by every count, has a larger population of wild animals, in winter, than any other area of comparable size not only in the country but perhaps on the continent. These graceful citizens move in toward Jackson roughly in concert with the outflung humans, perhaps trailing them a bit on the whole. They get restless when the first snow begins to stick to the high peaks, then as it moves progressively down the slopes of the mountains they keep just ahead of its descent until it flattens out over the valley floor, for keeps. Their job then is to make it through until spring, if they can —by no means all of them succeed—when they will reverse the movement and follow the greening grass back into the hills to the summer range and much happier days.

So all minds and all instincts, human and animal, now turn to thoughts of grub, in one direction or another: in a word, it's time to think of wintering, all hands anxious to eat something, or somebody. The cured grasses are rich in proteins and the hard tallow fat builds up under the hides of the ruminants to help them through the slim pickings to come. The little rodents store up seeds and the coyotes store up little rodents and the fat bear takes his winter in bed. The trout are winter-hungry and put on weight that makes them nicer to smoke; the wild ducks harvest the wild rice and the wild geese get plump and juicy on the white man's tame oats and the white man harvests everything but the coyote.*

It is quite a social time all around, everybody cooped up together, although of course the elk and the deer have no way of knowing, when they start down for the cocktail hour, that

* Bill Howard told of an old Indian chief who had worked up quite a reputation as a weather prophet around Blackfoot, Idaho. He was asked by a dude friend of Bill's what kind of winter it was going to be, in the mountains. The chief said it would be very cold, long, and generally tough. The dude was curious. "How do you know?" he asked. "Are the beaver making heap thick lodges?" The Indian shook his head. "Are the bank muskrats tunneling deeper?" Nope. "Have the geese got heap thick feathers on breast?" Hnn-nnh. "Then what is it?" the dude persisted. The old man shrugged. "White man putting in heap coal," he said.

a great many of them are going to end as the entrée, come dinner. In addition to these there are many bighorn sheep and moose, but the sheep stay higher up and the moose like to be by themselves in sequestered thickets and are not really any part of the community life.

The elk far outnumber all the other animals put together, for there are between 15,000 and 20,000 of them in the herd. About half of these gather on the U.S. Government Elk Refuge, which not only adjoins the town of Jackson but is, in a way of speaking, practically in it; for about half a mile the refuge fence and the town limits are the same, and the conformation of this is such that the refuge curves in almost to the town square itself. Since this part of the refuge is popular with the older and more sophisticated elk, especially the ancient and lordly bulls who can take their liquor or leave it alone, it's nothing for a couple of thousand of them to line up and stare down the outnumbered Jackson garrison, the members of which sometimes get mixed up about the situation, wondering just who is on which side of the fence.

Next to the elk in numbers are the deer. They are more friendly than the elk; they do not look in from behind any fence (or look out, whichever it is) but come right in and window-shop around the square or bed down in the little park. They are orderly and polite, and although Jim Varley still swears that an eight-point buck once bummed him for a dime in front of the RJ Bar, there is no record of a single deer ever having been booked into the jail. It seems a shame to eat such nice people.

Third in numbers probably are the coyotes, although there is no way of knowing for sure. If you depend upon sight to count them, there are no more than half a dozen in the entire Jackson Hole area, but if you go by sound alone there are at least a million. The high-keyed cry of just one of these babies sounds like fifty, and when they get to talking to each other on a calm moonlit autumn night, from hill to hill and from canyon to canyon, creek bed to creek bed and meadow to meadow, squads become companies and companies battalions and battalions divisions and divisions whole armies.

They don't all howl at once. A coyote in Cache Creek Canyon may start it, and this sets off all the others in that area, and now the refrain is picked up by the boys over on Flat Creek, passed on to the South Park crowd, which trills it all the way up the slope of Snow King Mountain, then the meadow larks—the lowland prowlers—come in, scattered rugged individuals yip it up, and just as the symphony seems played out Cache Creek swings in again and takes it from there, and the whole thing starts over.*

As winter wears on and pickings get slimmer they move in closer, and now comes the interminable cold war with the town's dogs, mostly at vocal range, but occasionally a coyote or two come right in, still giving voice. When this happens the dogs, who are fat Republicans, as against the coyotes, who vote the straight Democratic ticket, quickly scratch on the home doors, begging mama to open up.

The Jackson Hole elk reached the sanctuary and grub-line of the Government Elk Refuge only after many years of struggle for survival itself. When the first homesteaders came in and took up the valley bottomlands, there to raise domestic hay or cut wild hay and stack all of it in order to get their cattle through the winter, they were usurping the natural

* The nearest thing I ever have known to the shrill piping howl of the coyote is the high laugh of the loon (sometimes called the Great American Diver). Once when I was a United States Forest Service Ranger, on canoe patrol along the Minnesota-Canada border, in the Superior National Forest, I was teamed up with Oscar Heikilla, a state game warden. We got lost in the lower reaches of Little Saganaga Lake and couldn't decide in which direction lay Ogishkemuncie Lake, our next objective. That night at Oscar's suggestion we listened to the loons, and could hear them "talking" to each other, from lake to lake, and easily spotted Ogishkemuncie and made the portage without trouble the following morning.

winter range of the elk. The lush summer pastures in the interstices of the mountains can support an almost infinite number of ruminants, wild or tame, but the relatively tiny winter range, where the crust of winter is thinner and the heavy lowland grasses, with a little pawing, are available, is definitive in determining precisely how many head can be carried through.

So when the ranchers took this over the elk were left to go to bed without their supper, and many thousands of them starved: at one time, a full half of the herd in a single winter. But the elk made a fight of it. They not only crashed the fences that enclosed the haystacks, in an unbelievable combination of brute strength and animal cunning, against every defense the ranchers could put up, but mingled with the domestic stock in the feed lots, even chased horses from their stalls and took over.

With the fate of this great herd in the balance, in 1907 the state of Wyoming began some modest feeding, and in 1913 the Federal Government, through purchase of several ranches along Flat Creek, near Jackson, set up the National Elk Refuge. This 2,800-acre area was increased in size through various means and now the refuge covers about 25,000 acres, and the elk seems to be out of the woods, although about a thousand die there each winter in spite of all that can be done both in giving them room to forage for themselves and in feeding them liberally from the large store of hay and alfalfa that is grown on the refuge, plus tons of cottonseed cake that are brought in from outside.

During the hunting season an average of about four thousand elk are killed each year.

But the herd stays about the same.

The town of Jackson was built, or grew, squarely across the old path the elk used for moving from the upper part of the Hole to the lower part, and before the refuge fence was put up they kept using their ancient trail, right through town, and in winter the population was about half elk and half other people. The elk more or less ignored the interlopers, chasing horses out of barns and eating their grub, and more than once the town school had to be closed, toward spring, when big bull elk, who can be mean at that time of year, virtually took over the little settlement.

Now, as I have indicated, they are fenced off, admittance to the cocktail hour by invitation only, this invitation being, in their case, a metal tag that must be attached, post mortem, to each elk consumed.

During the winter of 1948–49, that terrific one that just about closed up the whole West and left Jackson Hole completely isolated for nearly a month, the elk herd rendered a rather special service to the community. Certain essential supplies, including medical ones, were badly needed and the lack of mail and news was distressing. The only way to bring these things in was by aircraft, but there was no place for a light plane to land in the deep soft snow, and the distances from usable airstrips elsewhere were too great to allow for a round trip without refueling, thus precluding an airdrop.

Communication by telephone fortunately was maintained. Roy Jensen was in Salt Lake City with his Cessna plane. He was told what was needed, and said he could take off in a few hours after being notified that landing facilities somehow or other had been set up for him in Jackson Hole. He didn't know how this could be done, the snow being what it was, and neither did anybody else, until Jack Francis happened to mention the circumstance to Almer Nelson, superintendent of the National Elk Refuge.

Almer had been on the job since 1923—he's still at it, in 1955—and he came up with the answer, which, it now seems in retrospect, anybody else could have come up with.

He and his helpers were feeding, heavily feeding, because

of the deep snow, around 8,000 elk on the refuge. The way this is done is to send out hayracks, horse-drawn, to circle over various parts of the area. From these the feed is tossed out onto the snow. Now Almer sent the hayracks out over one single path, about forty feet wide and a third of a mile long, and there they dumped their loads. Let the elk come in and get it. The elk did so. After two days of this, Almer sent the hayracks to another spot some distance away, to draw the elk in that direction.

Meantime, of course, the faithful animals had trampled down the snow to make a perfect landing strip, and Jensen was told about it. He flew in and, in a way of speaking, rescued the community.

He had medicine, mail, and essential supplies. He also had a five-gallon can of ice cream.

This was unloaded first of all.

No wonder the people of Jackson Hole are fond of the animals with whom they share the winter, either personally or at table.

Leave it to the elk.

chapter 7

Thanksgiving Almost Lays an Egg

EARLY in the morning of Thanksgiving Day, 1938, three Canada geese dropped out of the sky into the town of Jackson, dead. One fell at the edge of the town park, another hit a side street, the third landed exactly—give or take a few inches—on the doorstep of a house in which lived a family of five persons who through economic necessity had reconciled themselves to a bit of boiling beef for their holiday dinner and were mighty glad to have even that.

These geese each had been hit with pellets of No. 2 or No. 00 shot by hunters out near the Elk Refuge and had flown at least a half a mile before succumbing and tumbling to earth.

Flat Creek meanders through the refuge area, broad and sluggish, bordered by swampy areas, and the geese rest here, and do some feeding, as they come through the Hole on their way south from wherever they have been, and because of the conformation of the tall hills on either side they have to funnel out over the town, or close to it. Since geese do about 90 per cent of their honking upon taking off, and just afterwards, while they are trying to decide who is in charge, and other matters of goose protocol, the cocktail hour resounds to their morning babble, almost always at hours when decent people have just passed out.

A good many of the local citizens consider goose shooting to be the foremost sport of the year, and in times past a roast goose was thought of as the one and only Thanksgiving delicacy, or what all America calls The Bird. I shot my first ones back in 1925 with Doc Huff and Dick Winger. When the geese started to come through we anticipated some fine shooting out on the meadows north of town and along the Flat Creek bottoms, but a heavy fall of snow came along and we stood out in sinister silhouette against it. Doc solved this by pre-empting some operating gowns from the hospital. Included were the white hoods, "boots," the whole sterile works, and after he deftly and professionally had wound our shotguns with bandages we were able to sit in the snow, invisible even to the geese, and take our pick of the choicest morsels that flew over.

In recent years, however, an aura of pseudo-New York sophistication has hovered over the bridge-playing side of town and among other innovations in the art of delicate living introduced by this crust has been that of having turkey for Thanksgiving, thus tying in with the rest of the United States, including the Pilgrims.

The proletariat at first demurred, pointing out with disgusting logic that the reason the turkey was the Thanksgiving fowl was because the hungry and discouraged Pilgrims had shot them on the hoof, in the wild state, for they were native to that historic area, the same as the geese were in Jackson Hole. But presently even the most stubborn historians began to feel out of things unless they had turkey. The children would come home from school, weeping, water running through the dirt of their cheeks. "Ma," they'd say, "all the rich kids are having turkey and making faces at us." *

That settled it; the turkey now is ensconced as the Jackson Hole version of the life terrific.

This gesture on the side of culture has serious drawbacks,

* At Nino's Restaurant, in New York City, which specializes in wild-game dinners, a Thanksgiving repast built around a whole wild goose, for six persons, comes to $72.50. An identical meal, substituting a turkey for the goose, can be had for the price of the vegetables and the mince pie. The turkey is free.

making it even more attractive. Since turkeys are foreign to the Hole, they have to be imported from outside, and a long way outside, at that, and of course at a time of year when both Teton Pass and Hoback Canyon are subject to such traffic hazards as snowslides, deep drifts, ice, blizzards, and other routine calamities, which makes it hard to pinpoint the arrival of a truck or anything else in Jackson. Orders for turkeys, therefore, are taken way ahead of time, as far back as October, by the two butchershops in town, so that this delicacy can be delivered as near to Thanksgiving as possible.

Starting several days before the big Thursday feast in that winter of 1948 the elements gave the Hole a modest preview of what soon was to come. The advance storms were not enough to stop traffic completely, but one of them certainly hit the turkey-lift right in the breastbone.

The fowl for the smaller of the two stores had been brought in safely from Salt Lake City about three days in advance of the holiday, but the truck carrying those for the larger store came up against a major snowslide in Hoback Canyon, twenty miles south of town, in the early morning of the day before Thanksgiving. It ran off the road and was balanced on what I suppose we can designate as the brink of the precipice, or whatever they call the thing on television.

Anyway, it was stopped.

This disconcerting news came in by telephone from either a ranch house or a ranger station, I can't remember which, where the truck driver had taken refuge. It seemed clear that the truck, even with the help of all the highway equipment available, plus all volunteer assistance that could be rounded up, would not be able to make it in time. It also was pretty well established that a sort of bucket brigade made up of snowshoers and skiers could not transport the turkeys across the slide.

Jackson, as a whole, went into a state of turmoil, and the

inevitable choosing up of sides began. Those whose turkeys were on the wrong side of the snowslide wanted to postpone Thanksgiving for at least one day, most likely two. Those who had their turkeys were adamant, pointing out that the pies were baked and relatives had come in from distant ranches, and anyway Thanksgiving was Thanksgiving.

As it happened, the smaller store, whose truck had got through, catered mostly to the Republicans, who felt that not to have Thanksgiving in concert with Maine and Vermont was next to sacrilege. The Democrats, outnumbering the others and favoring the larger store, whose truck was down in Hoback Canyon, feverishly brought the attention of the others to the fact that President Roosevelt once had advanced the date of Thanksgiving for a much lesser reason than this. Why couldn't it be done again?

The Republicans pretended they never had heard of any Roosevelt this side of Teddy, and stuck to it, and won.

Both butchers almost instantly sold all the hamburger they had in stock, or quickly could grind up, for a hamburger flurry swept through town on the wings of the snow-laden wind. Part of this rush, of course, was propaganda. If the turkey-owning people would not deign to postpone Thanksgiving for a day or so, let their consciences comfort them. The others would eat, not wild goose or steak or perhaps chicken, but hamburger. In a word, let the Republicans in their bellyful after-dinner nap be disturbed by uneasy dreams of the Democrats and their hamburger, and see if that would help their digestion any.

Another reason for the hamburger run was more on the realistic side. There still was a chance that the second turkey truck somehow would manage to get through in time, so the hamburger was looked at not as a certainty for Thanksgiving dinner but in the nature of a hedge. Nobody wanted to hedge with anything as expensive as steak, or canned ham, the turkey already having used up the November meat budget.

Well, on Thanksgiving morning a certain thing happened.

What was it?

Did the Republicans finally give in and postpone the holiday, unbelievable as this may seem?

Did the truck make it through?

What *really* occurred?

Don't go to sleep yet—read the next chapter.

chapter 8

The Kangaroo-Hide Boots

I WAS standing at the Silver Dollar bar talking with Joe Fussey, a former cowboy now dealing blackjack, craps, and roulette in the gambling room, discussing—as who wasn't?—the big news of this day before Thanksgiving; namely, the turkey truck that had been held up down in the Hoback.*

Art Jones came along and joined us. Art was a young rancher and breeder of horses, specializing in that Western standby, the quarter-horse, a cross of the Morgan horse (U.S. Cavalry) and the Arabian (thoroughbred racer) that adds up to the finest cowpony in the world. He was relatively new in Jackson Hole, having come up from Pinedale, Wyoming, two years before, and had a ranch near town. I knew Art by sight but not personally. He now introduced himself to me—he and Joe plainly were old friends—and said, "If you haven't already signed up someplace else, Phronia and I would be very pleased if you would have Thanksgiving dinner with us tomorrow. Joe is coming down."

I was alone, and this invitation from a virtual stranger, given in a certain casual Western way that precluded any thought of my being a charity patient or of this being a gesture by a do-gooder, I thought was one of the nicest things that had happened to me in a long time. Done in any

* In the American West, all men handling games for the house are known as dealers. Elsewhere a man presiding over the roulette wheel is called a croupier, and of course there is no such thing, actually, as "dealing" craps. But anyway, for no reason that I know of, the generic term "dealer" holds.

other way I might have been offended, but it so plainly was—if I may use the word again—nice that I accepted at once.

Art joined in our conversation about the turkey truck. Joe thought that perhaps an effort would be made to carry the precious cargo across the slide, but Art thought not. "You can't monkey around with a slide," he said. "This is just a little one, as I get it, and the main thing is that the truck is off the road, but the smallest slide is too big to take a chance with, because you might set it to running again and they could find your body in the spring."

Their own turkeys, Art said—two of them—were in the truck, but he had shot a couple of wild geese and if the truck didn't make it that was what we would have. Although it didn't make any difference to him, therefore, one way or another, he took a position with respect to having Thanksgiving a day late that was the same as that held by Joe and me. The hamburger run was on at the moment, the whole town seething.

"What the hell," Art said, "we're a long way from everyplace, and a day doesn't make any difference. The truck might get in a day late, but the whole town could eat turkey at the same time. That's what Thanksgiving is for."

It was startling to find three people together, at the same time, who agreed on this subject, or for that matter any other subject. An historic moment, in Jackson Hole.

We arranged to meet at the bar at two o'clock the next day, when Art would drive us out to the ranch. We had another beer, then Art went on home and it was time for Joe to go on duty and I walked over to the crap table with him and quickly lost all the money I had in my pocket, plus a couple bucks on credit, then had my dinner and went to bed early and read until late. I came into the bar on Thanksgiving just after noon and Joe was there and he had the big news——

The turkey truck, with the help of Highway Department equipment, somehow or other had managed to get through and had arrived in town early in the morning.

It certainly was a relief; you could feel it in the air.

Presently Art drove up with his Pontiac car and came in and we had a quick one and then he took us down to the ranch, which was on Cache Creek three miles below town.

Twelve persons, besides Joe and me, were on hand for the Thanksgiving dinner. All were relatives or old family friends; six were children of various ages. Phronia Jones, Art's wife, and if I may say so an extraordinarily pretty girl, had started her dinner a few days, in some respects weeks, before. Art had shot an elk and a deer, besides the geese and some ducks, and while the animals were being cut up for freezing and hanging in a shed for the winter Phronia had selected the cuts she wanted for her mince meat and her suet pudding. She then had made these mixtures and placed them in a cool kitchen cupboard for settling and aging.

The visiting women helped Phronia with the last-minute cooking and the table routine and the men gathered in the living room and presently started a poker game for small stakes. Then just before time for dinner, the house loaded with the smell of roast turkey (I still wished we could have had wild goose), the distaff side now came in and we had a great surprise: two magnums of Moët & Chandon champagne. This, Phronia explained, was a present from Wilford Neilson, publisher of the Jackson's Hole *Courier*, and it had come about as follows:

About a month before, Phronia was driving the pickup truck through Dry Gulch and she came on Wilford, in his car. He was in trouble; his automobile was stuck, the wheels spinning because of ice in the ruts of the dirt road. Phronia got out and looked the situation over and decided he needed some gravel. She got a shovel from her truck and found some unfrozen gravel and sluiced it under the rear tires, telling Wilford to rock the car gently while she was doing it. It worked.

Soon after that Phronia and Art were in town for their wedding anniversary, having dinner at the hotel, and Wilford came along and told Art how Phronia had helped him, then he went away and came back with three bottles of champagne that some dude had given him the summer before, or two summers before, and they had lain forgotten under a pile of old *Couriers*, as Wilford wasn't much of a champagne drinker. They opened one and drank it to the anniversary, then Wilford gave them the other two for Thanksgiving. So we had them now. Art opened the bottles and Phronia poured, giving each of the children a small sip too. We made toasts and had a gay time.

During this interlude the center of interest, next to the champagne, was Joe Fussey's new pair of boots. Joe was the only one of us who dressed up, although he couldn't really be called dressed up because he had on what he wore every day: a large white Stetson, a beautifully tailored light-green Pendleton shirt with white pearl buttons down the front and on the pockets and along the cuffs, a little feathery yellow tie, a pair of mauve Western pants perfectly fitted, and his boots.

This getup was very effective during the dude season, in respect to his trade, but it really was no pose on Joe's part. He had been a cowboy for years on Montana and Wyoming ranges before he took up gambling as a profession, and he had the cowboy's love of having fine things, never mind the cost, just so they were in good taste, a refinement of the working clothes ordinarily worn.*

* The cowboy's regalia is the only folk dress known in North America, in the sense that he wears it as the badge of his trade when—so to speak—off duty, and takes pride in it. This is based, perhaps, on the fact that everything he wears is functional. Glen Dyrland, a cowboy employed at the V-V

The boots we all now were looking at were beauties, undoubtedly the best in the Hole as of that moment. They were made of pure-white kid and brown kangaroo in the usual intricate Western design, nicely pointed and perfectly modeled, obviously an expensive custom job. In fact Joe told us they had set him back $70, made in Salt Lake. We took turns feeling the soft pliability of the tops and the wonderful glovelike fit and firmness over the instep: when Joe flexed his toes you could feel, and even see, the ripple of the tendons under the leather. Art Jones said they were the best boots he ever had seen in his life.

Presently we went in to dinner. I don't recall all that we had to eat; perhaps it's enough to say that it was a Thanksgiving feast in the full-blown tradition, many more things than anybody could eat even in token portions. Then the women cleared the table of everything but the remains of the turkeys and a few other items that could be nibbled at, by hand, should anybody be hungry later: an incredible supposition, but dear to the female heart.

By now it was dark out, and Art and the other men went out into the deep snow (Joe had overshoes to pull on over his boots) to see how the horses were doing, or to bring them into the barn, or something else. I was too full of turkey to ask. They were gone a long time, and during their absence the women, experts in their own field, miraculously managed not only to dispose of the dishes but to get the younger of the kids, at least, to bed. Major accomplishment. Having nothing to do, I just sat there alone and reviewed my life, wishing I knew enough about horses to help the others, but still comforting myself with the thought that, hell being paved

---

ranch just south of Hoback Canyon, and not a dude wrangler, once had a pair of chaps that cost him $65, a saddle that he paid $200 for, a Navajo saddle blanket at $25, a $50 bridle, and a pair of boots that set him back $125. This was no show; he was not on parade. He just spent his wages that way because he wanted to.

with amateur cowboys, I at least knew enough to keep out of the way.

By nine o'clock, I should judge, the men were back and everything was in order, outside and inside. We talked for a couple of hours and then, some of the party having got up at dawn, we came to the end of still one more Thanksgiving day. Art and Phronia and Art's brother, Eddie, and Claude Wham, a rancher from up on the Gros Ventre, drove Joe and me back to town.

As we were about to pass Roy Jensen's bar, Joe and I asked the others in for a nightcap. So we parked the car and went in and had a couple of rounds of beers and talked about our Thanksgiving and about the turkeys having been got in. Roy had some further dope on this: how the plow had nudged the slide and found it firm, then all hands had walked across it and slowly had transferred the turkeys, and the lightened truck was able to creep over.

Some one of us noticed that the poker table in the corner was not being used. Somebody said, "Maybe we ought to go on with that game a little bit," referring back to the casual nickel-and-dime thing we had filled in time with before dinner.

We took our glasses over to the table and Roy turned on the light above it and gave us some cards and we began playing. It was quarters at first but as we went along the stakes rose as inevitably as yeast rises in a loaf of pregnant dough and pretty soon it cost a couple of bucks just to look.

It presently became plain that the play was between Art and Joe Fussey. Claude dropped, and Phronia took $10 away and bought us all a drink with it, and I stayed around a while but had to let it go. Those of us who were out watched the contest between Art and Joe, and some others from the bar came around. Roy Jensen sat down and acted as banker. Art kept winning, but Joe made a nice comeback for a while and it looked as though he might take over, but then it leveled off and was even for a long time, give-and-take. Art apparently got tired of this and ran a very neat bluff on a hole card, and things turned his way; he pressed on, and it wasn't long before Joe was on the ropes and hanging there: everything he tried went wrong, and when he was nearly out of money they decided on one final hand and call it a night, as Phronia was very sleepy.

Right from the start, Joe seemed to have this one sewed up. This hand. I'll not go through it, because I can't remember it, but he apparently had Art on the hook with possible kings back to back; anyway, he played it that way, with a king showing. Then he got a low pair on the board, and Art got a bigger pair. On the final card Art made a nominal bet and Joe raised and Art quickly covered it and shoved in fifty dollars more, cash on the line.

Joe thought this over for a few minutes. He could have put in the rest of his chips, amounting I suppose to around twenty dollars, for a cut of the pot in that amount should he win, but instead he reached down and took off his boots. He said, "We wear the same size, Art. Try them on."

Art pulled off his loose-fitting old decrepit corral boots, a couple of wrecks for sure, and tried on Joe's elegant pair. He got up and walked around the room, and felt of the boots with his hands. Then he sat down and looked at Joe and nodded.

"Okay," Joe said, "I'll put them in for fifty dollars, provided I get your old boots in the bargain, if I lose. I can't walk to the hotel barefoot."

Art agreed. Slowly they turned over their hole cards.

Art had three of a kind and Joe Fussey no longer had a pair of fancy boots . . .

They let us out at the hotel and Joe and I said good night

to the others, thanking them all, then stopped at the Silver Dollar Bar for a final one.

Slim Linville, the night marshal, was there.

"Slim," I said, "they got those turkeys through."

"It was a miracle," Slim said. "They did everything wrong. They took a chance I wouldn't take if I live to be a million. Of course," he added, tilting his hat and scratching his head, "it worked out."

"That's the answer," I said, and Slim laughed. He turned away toward the door. "Not much to do tonight," he said, "everybody full of turkey, but I got to look around."

Joe and I lifted our beers. "I'm sorry about your boots," I said.

He looked at me in a curious way. I can't describe it exactly, it was a mixture of amusement, surprise, and a sort of incredulity. "Why?" he asked.

"They were wonderful boots," I said uncomfortably, realizing that in some way I was out of my element but not knowing what else to say.

Joe looked down at Art's old boots and made little movements of his feet as though feeling them out. "Nothing wrong with these," he said. "As a matter of actual fact," he went on, sipping his beer, "wait till Art tries to keep that white leather clean. I was worrying a little about that myself. Another thing, those boots were a little tight across the instep for me. They were just right for Art. I could see it."

We finished our beers and had one more.

"However it is," Joe said as we turned from the bar, "Art beat me the poker hand. I've won and lost a million poker hands. It goes one way or another way. Art had me clean beat, a nice hand, he played it right. You couldn't lose a pair of boots to a nicer human guy than Art Jones."

I said it wasn't likely you could, and we said good night.

chapter 9

My Cabin

EARLY in the fall I had decided to stay in Jackson at least for the winter and possibly longer, and to this end I felt I ought to have a town residence, something on the order of a Park Avenue penthouse, conveniently located close to the business and social center of the community. A view of the mountains, if possible. As a major consideration, on the economic level, I then could prepare my own meals and also, as a major consideration on the same level, the probable rent, as against hotel living, would be in my favor.

However, the housing shortage in Jackson is chronic. Through the summer every place is taken, far in advance, by the incoming gamblers and other tourist-season workers, and in the fall, when these leave, the houses—there never are many available—are filled by the incoming ranchers and others who want to winter in town.

I placed my problem before Willard Miner, which roughly was comparable to taking a full-page ad in the paper, and the next day he told me about a log cabin, nearby, then occupied by Ann LaSalle, a blackjack dealer at the Cowboy, and her husband, Bobby, a former top-ranking middleweight (something like 22 knockouts in around 70 bouts), between Pat Patterson's house and the high school. Willard thought that Bobby and Ann would be pulling out for Reno soon.

First I cased the joint, and it was wonderful, from the outside. It was set far back from the street—more a road than a street—virtually in Pat Patterson's back yard, no more than thirty feet from the croquet layout he kept up for the lady shills and cocktail waitresses who lived with him, and on the other side it faced the high school athletic field, a large vacant lot. The orientation of the cabin with the rest of the town just about took my breath away. It was a short block from the Silver Dollar, less than two from the Log Cabin, and a hundred feet more from both the RJ and the Cowboy. It would have been hard to find a place, unless it was on the square itself, so sensationally situated. (It also was within walking distance, supposing one to feel energetic, of the grocery stores, the post office, and other establishments of routine academic interest.)

It was a little old log cabin, small and squat and bulging a little and tired, something on the order of the one in which Lincoln was born—which, although I do not feel that I resemble Lincoln personally, I thought quite interesting. I found later that it had been built on a homestead north of Flat Creek, a great many years ago, and in 1920 had been moved into town. It was almost surrounded by tin cans, a lot of bottles (empty), and many elk bones without—I discovered—any edible meat on them. And so on.

I went over to the Cowboy to see Ann. She was busy dealing, but Bobby was at the bar—he was shilling the crap table, which at the moment was not getting any play—and I asked him about the cabin and he said everything was up to Ann. When she was through working I went over to her and asked her about it.

"Well, I'll tell you, Don," she said, riffling the cards, "we may stay in for the hunting and we may not. If things look up, we may stay on until the first of the year. Things are slow over at Reno, not hot at all, and what the hell. However it is, we have nothing to say about who gets the cabin. It belongs to Willie Kuhrtz. Willie has a key, and it's okay with me to have you go inside and take a look. It's a peach of a cabin and I hope you get it."

I knew Willie Kuhrtz very well, but didn't know he owned any cabin. He was an expert cabinetmaker, a wonderful craftsman, and at the moment he was putting in some panels at the RJ. I went over there and told him I understood the cabin would be available when Bobby and Ann left.

He stopped work and we had a beer.

"Sure," he said, "it's for rent. Sixty a month, completely furnished, linen and all the rest."

"Let's go look at it," I said, "and if I like it I'll give you forty a month."

"It's a deal," Willie said.

He hadn't a key because, he explained, the cabin really wasn't his, but belonged to his wife, Nancy, who had gone to Indiana for the winter to visit her folks. She had rented it to the LaSalles, handled the whole thing. So we went to the Cowboy and got the key from Ann, and walked over to the cabin.

"This junk will all be hauled away," he said, waving an arm to take in the yard. He pointed to Pat's croquet court. "Floor show all summer, or as long as you stay after May," he said. "The girls play a wonderful game. The accepted uniform is a bra and a pair of panties. Main window of the cabin looks right out on it. Beautiful shills, cocktail waitresses, and so on. I ought to get fifty a month."

"Forty," I said, and we moved to the cabin. Two steps led up to the door, and when Willie stepped on the first one it collapsed. He shrugged off this minor incident.

"Never mind," he said generously, evidently under the impression that I was about to apologize for the condition of the step. "Soon as the snow comes you won't know whether you got a bottom step or not. Entirely covered over, just in the way. Nobody needs one."

We went inside. The interior of the cabin was as ordered

and neat as its exterior and its immediate surroundings, were decayed and littered. This circumstance was quite in keeping with the general idea in Jackson. Here the clean white hand of winter lies over everything for much of the year, and the bankrupt yard of one person's dwelling under this benign blanket looks exactly the same as that of the banker, who has balanced his aesthetic budget with a plot of fancy grass and a well-trimmed hedge. But for a very long time all yards, tin-canned or flowered, look the same; all that counts is the inside of the house.

The cabin consisted of one room, about twelve by eighteen feet. At one end of the room was an oil heater, also the kitchen and dining area, just off the area, which was eighteen inches away, as the crow flies. At the opposite end was a closet and the bathroom, which included a shower stall and a hot-water heater. The cabin as a whole was beautifully finished in native pine trim, obviously by Willie's own practiced hand, and wallboard. The floor was covered with a red figured linoleum. Everything was spotless.

"Willie," I said, "I'll take it."

He said, "Oh, hell, don't be in such a rush. I haven't half showed it to you yet. Try the bed." I tried it; it was fine. Willie pointed around at various things. "Pressure cooker, dishes, utensils, linen, electric hotplate, everything you need. Convenient electric plugs; I did all the wiring myself, you'll notice it's concealed. I'll put in a new cupboard for you. Could you use a typewriter table? I'll make you one in no time." He snapped his fingers. "By the way, do you like elk meat?"

"Yes," I said.

"Well, I tell you what I'll do. I'll bring you an elk steak once a week. Fridays, let's say. Friday okay with you?" I said Friday was fine, and he asked, "How thick do you like your elk steaks?"

"Two inches," I said.

He rubbed his nose. "That's too thick for elk. An inch is a mighty fine thickness but I suppose I could make it an inch and a quarter, say. Inch and a half on occasion."

I thought it over. "In consideration of the elk," I said, "I believe I could arrange to keep my rent paid two months in advance. Nothing like a good thick elk steak."

Willie squinted. "You mean two inches, don't you?"

"In a way," I said.

He waved a hand. "She's two inches. Let's go over and have a drink to celebrate the whole deal."

We went back to the RJ and after we'd celebrated with a few Willie said, "You know, maybe we ought to have some kind of lease, in writing, both of us sign it." He got a pencil and a piece of paper from Jack Francis and wrote it out. He signed it, and gave it to me to sign. He had put down the rent at forty, this to be two months in advance on a steady basis; the cabin completely furnished; one elk steak, inch and a half thick, per week.

"Willie," I said, "you've got it an inch and a half."

"Don't pay any attention to that," he said quickly. "I'll cut it full. Suppose it says two inches and my knife slips a little, damn it I have broken the whole lease." He finished his drink. "We could make it read two inches and put in there 'allowing for normal shrinkage.' "

I finished my drink. "All right," I said, "but in that case where it says two months rent in advance on a 'steady' basis, make it on a 'reasonable' basis."

"God damn it," Willie said, "are all leases as complicated as this?" He penciled in the changes and we initialed them, and I signed it. He put it in his shirt pocket and ordered another drink for us.

"How about my copy of the lease?" I asked.

Willie looked at me. "You mean you don't trust me?" he asked in a hurt tone of voice. "Have you got a filing cabinet?"

I said I hadn't one. He said, "Well, I have. Over at the shop. I'll put this lease in it. Under L, for lease. Or maybe C, for cabin. In any case we're all set, everything in order, the whole thing strictly legal. Here's a go."

I spent the next few weeks of my life telling Bobby and Ann LaSalle interesting stories about how tough the winter could be in Jackson Hole, starting right now.

"The damn thing comes in around this time in the fall," I explained, "and the first thing you know you can't get out until spring. You never can tell. It's none of my business, but if the two of you want to go to Reno this winter, I'd suggest you don't take any chances. Get going."

To my delight the snow began to sift in. The hunting season was on late that year, and Ann was getting a good play, and so was the crap table, and this annoyed me, because I wanted my cabin. I stepped up the intensity of my accounts of people getting snowed in for the winter. I invented stories that were hard for even me to believe. I told Ann, "Ann, if you and Bobby can still get out, you're lucky."

They hung on.

I would walk past my future home, looking at it as a younger person, or an older person, might look at Marilyn Monroe. That cabin, its littered yard now a pristine white, was a beautiful thing to see.

One night a mild blizzard moved in. I hurried over to the Cowboy. "Ann," I said, "you and I and Bobby have always been friends." I leaned toward her and spoke out of the side of my mouth. "Get out!"

Two days later I found a note left for me at the Wort Hotel by Bobby LaSalle. They had left during the night. Willie had the key. So long, and good luck.

I couldn't find Willie at first so I went over to Mercill's Store and exuberantly ordered a large stock of groceries and supplies, these to be delivered at the cabin later in the day. Presently I found Willie at Roy Jensen's and he gave me the key. "You'll be as snug as a bug in a rug over there," he said. "I'm going hunting and the minute I get back——" He held his thumb and forefinger an inch and a half apart, and winked at me happily. The elk steak.

I took the key over to the cabin and entered. The place was as clean as could be and good little Ann, as fine a housekeeper as a blackjack table ever produced, had left me seventeen kinds of spices, nearly a quart of olive oil, some sleeping pills, a dozen eggs, some red nail lacquer, half a pound of bacon, and a selection of condiments. Fresh linen lay folded upon the bed.

In a word, I was at home.

At this point I happened to glance at my kitchen table, and the shelves beneath it. These things seemed singularly empty. A quick and sickening survey disclosed that I had no knife, no fork, no spoon; I had no dishes of any kind. No pots, no pans, no nothing, not even a hotplate to cook on.

In a word, I was destitute.

I sat on the edge of my bed for a while, then decided to go out and try to find Willie. It was chilly in the cabin and I thought I would light my heater so it would be warm when I returned, whenever that might be. It wouldn't start. The only response I got was a slow dripping of oil onto the cabin floor. Since I couldn't find out where it came from, I had to give up trying to light the stove, for fear I would light the whole cabin. I tried the hot-water heater, but the pilot light was out and I didn't know how to start it.

At this point my groceries arrived. With some bitterness, and with no little damage to the big toe of my right foot, I kicked the two cartons into a corner and went out and over to Willie's shop. It was closed. I went to the Cowboy and Willie had just left, and I went to Roy's and Willie had just left.

Briefly, I could not find Willie, but I did find out that he was leaving for Joe Madden's hunting camp with Joe, for a ten-day stay, sometime during the night. I tried to find Joe but couldn't find him.

I waited around for Willie in all the bars until they closed and the only place open was Bob McGee's lunch counter. Willie wasn't there and I had some coffee with Charlotte Simons, the handsome night waitress, then decided to return to my new cabin and go to bed. It was raining out, and the night was perfectly black. There were no lights anywhere. Pat Patterson's house, wherever it was, was dark. I couldn't locate the high school. In a word, I was unable to find my cabin. I went back to the lunchroom to see if Charlotte had a flashlight, but she hadn't any. On the back of a menu she drew me a rough map and I tried it again, but still the cabin eluded me. I returned to the lunchroom and drank a few cups of coffee, chatting with Charlotte, and at dawn the rain let up and the sky got gray and I went out and of course walked directly to my cabin, which, apparently, had been there all the time. I saw certain footprints, washed out in part but unmistakable, marking the course of somebody who had been wandering around on the school athletic field and various other places and at one point had stumbled over a log about ten feet from my cabin. I remembered stumbling over the log . . .

I went to bed and slept until nearly noon, then resumed my hunt for Willie. His shop, as it had been the night before, was padlocked, and since he lived in quarters in the rear of the shop there was no way of finding out if he was there when the front was closed. I ran into Jack Banning (impresario of the office party, you remember,) and he said that Willie and Joe had left for the hills. A chill wind had come up, the temperature was well below freezing, and I told Jack about my nonlightable heater. He said he knew all about oil heaters and we went to the cabin and in the twinkling of an eye—which in Jackson Hole means anything from two hours to a week—he got the thing working. He could not, however, figure out the pilot light in the hot-water heater. I should worry about that. That was just for a shower and shaving and I could, and still can, go without both just as long as anybody in Teton County could, or can.

Now that I was warm, I got along fine on cold groceries and five days later I saw a familiar figure on the street, going away.

"Hi!" I called. "Willie!"

He turned around and came back to meet me. "I've been up in camp," he said, "and I've got to go back tonight for a few days. Don't worry about the elk steak." He held thumb and forefinger about $1\frac{5}{16}$ inches apart. "Soon as I get back."

"Willie," I said, "I'm not worried about that. The thing of it is, there's no use having any elk steak if you can't cook it. Of course I could cook it in the back yard, but I have no knife, no fork, no spoon. Looking at it one way, of course you don't need any knife or fork or spoon. No plate. Let's see . . . naturally, you don't need a plate. But look, Willie, I just haven't anything at all. No electric hotplate, no saucepans, no skillet . . ." And I went on to mention all the things that apparently had been there before but were not there now.

Willie looked puzzled. "It was all there," he said vaguely. "I wonder . . . Of course some of it could have belonged to Bobby and Ann. Like I told you, Nancy handled everything. In any case, everything I have, along that line, is up at the hunting camp. How about some more blankets? Look, I'll run down in the jeep the day after tomorrow. About noon. Shall we say a quarter to one?"

"Ten minutes to one," I said.

Willie snapped his fingers. "On the nose," he said.

Ten days later, toward the end of a beautiful fall day, Willie showed up, out of breath, lugging a large carton. He came in and put it on the table. "There!" he cried.

I looked into the carton. It contained a lot of crockery, glasses, and some silverware, as it technically is called. I took everything out. There were nine plates, sixteen table knives, eleven saucers, three cups, and a large cracked bowl.

"I brought it all down from the hunting camp," Willie said. "We're all set."

"I don't know," I said gently, trying not to hurt my friend's feelings. "What do you expect me to do with nine plates? Remember, I have only one bed. And there's nothing here to cook with. Where's my hotplate? How about a skillet? Have you got a Dutch oven? Maybe you could let me have . . ." I searched for the right word. "I need a hunting knife."

Willie looked discouraged. "I've got so many things on my mind I don't know if I'm coming or going," he said. "I got to make a bedroom set for some people in Enid, Oklahoma."

"I need an ax," I said. "And the pilot light in the hot-water heater doesn't work. Jack Banning tried to fix it."

"Jesus H. Christ!" Willie said, moving his hands around. He looked at his watch. "I don't know when I've been so busy. But maybe I can fix that pilot light right now, if it doesn't take too long." He went out into the little bathroom and I could hear him grunting and swearing. He came back and sat down. "I need a wrench," he said. "Look, why do we have to be in such a rush about everything? People these days don't know how to take it easy, and they die of heart attacks. Let's just sit here a while, have a couple of drinks, and talk things over like gentlemen."

At first I was stunned. Then I remembered that behind some heavy curtains at the bathroom window I had put a bottle of whiskey, on the sill to keep it cool. I said, "Willie, you have a much better eye when looking around the bathroom than you have when you're looking at the things I haven't got around here." I got the whiskey and poured a couple.

"Now," Willie said, "just give me a pencil and one of those scratch pads, there." I did so. "Let's get organized," he said. "I want this to be the finest place you ever lived in in your life." He drank most of his drink and poised the pencil. "Number one!" he cried.

"Pilot light, hot-water heater," I said.

"Number one: pilot light! Next!"

"Electric hotplate."

We went through thirteen items, all carefully numbered and noted by Willie.

When we came to a possible fourteenth item, I mentioned the idea of boarding up the bathroom window, from the outside, in the interest of warmth for the winter.

"I'd be glad to do that," Willie said thoughtfully, "but I wouldn't suggest it. Sometimes in mild weather you might like some outdoor light in there, and in really cold weather those curtains will handle your problem, if you keep them drawn together. Perfect insulation. Do you know what those curtains are?"

"No," I said; "but you saw the whiskey through them."

"I did not. I drew them apart for more light. Those are blackout curtains from a British battleship. I got them when I was in the merchant marine, in the North Atlantic. You can't tell me anything about blackout curtains from a British battleship."

"I'm not trying to," I said.

"Well, don't try. Now that brings up a different subject. I can get you a cannon."

"A what?" I said.

"A cannon. Forty-millimeter. I have a friend in the Navy,

in Seattle, who has been wanting to send me a forty-millimeter cannon ever since the end of the war."

"I don't think I need a cannon," I said. "If I could just get the pilot light on the hot-water heater to work——"

"Forget that," Willie said. "It's as good as done. It's down here on the list, isn't it? Coming back to the cannon, we have a big front yard here, between here and the road, and the cannon might look all right."

"Would it be larger or smaller than the cabin?" I asked.

Willie scratched his head. "You can't compare the two," he said, "because of the terrific difference in shape. One way the cabin would be bigger, and another way the cannon would be. In any case, if you didn't think it looked right, you could always pawn it."

He made a note to write to Seattle. "Incidentally," he asked, "do you like Chinese food?"

"Yes," I said.

"Fine. I've got three pairs of chopsticks over at the shop. A Chinese dinner without chopsticks isn't a Chinese dinner. I'll bring them over. Chopsticks," he muttered, making a note. He rattled the pencil between his teeth. "How about an Oriental rug?" I nodded. He put it down. "I have three," he said. Now another thing you need is a box nailed up outside your door where you can keep things frozen, in the winter. I'll fix one for you, with shelves and door, and I'll also put up the shelves inside, here." He put away his notes. "Well, I've got to run. See you tomorrow, and we'll get right to work."

"Maybe I ought to have a copy of that list," I said.

Willie shrugged. "Forget it," he said. "I'll file it in my filing cabinet, right along with the lease." I went to the door with him. We stood for a moment on the top step. It was a beautiful evening. A flock of pintail ducks flew past, a lovely sight against the dark yellowing sky. Some mallards passed them, lower, in the opposite direction, going up Flat Creek.

"A wonderful country," Willie said. "And in the early summer, the croquet game, with all the beautiful . . . You know, I think I ought to get sixty——"

"Forty," I said.

"Okay," Willie said. "Well, good night." He stepped onto the lower step, the broken one, and nearly fell. Recovering with incredible dexterity, he waved a hand and walked away, slowly. I heard some geese, out on the Elk Refuge, giving voice, and knew they soon would come past. Mingled with this came another sound. It was Willie, on his way to the Silver Dollar.

He was singing *Home on the Range.*

I've never heard it sung better . . .

chapter 10

The Children's Hour

JACKSON Hole, as everyplace else seems to, has its troubles with what loosely is referred to as "juvenile delinquency," a term of broad convenience, but here it takes a somewhat different form from that of, say, New York.

There are not many opportunities around here for the legitimate New York article, the real thing. In warm weather, especially when the dude season is on and the pretty dude girls just about stagger the imagination, the fences surrounding the park are well lined each evening with hopeful and potential juvenile delinquents thirstily watching the proceedings, ticking off on their fingers the years before they will be allowed in the palaces of sin across the street without having to be accompanied by parents or other wet blankets, but this doesn't add up to much.

What adds up is the fiendish practice of these kids in going out fishing, hunting, camping, and otherwise engaging in unwholesome undertakings. When winter comes it is skiing, and this is the worst thing of all.

One day between Christmas and New Year's I noticed that all four saloons had slotted tin cans on the bars with a superimposed legend, KEEP THE YOUNG FOLKS INDOORS! This puzzled me somewhat, because not too long before that I reluctantly had donated to similar cans on New York bars for the purpose, so the sign said, of getting the kids out of the indoors and way to the hell and gone into the outdoors, away from the pool halls and streets and bowling alleys and other places in which amateur sociologists think crime breeds.*

I asked Willard Miner about the can on his bar.

"Well, I tell you," he said, "I think the committee has got a pretty good idea. They want to have a place here in town where they can put in a few pool tables, maybe a bowling alley, pinball, and other nice things for the kids of this town. Nice clean recreation. The way it is now, they go out and set fire to the woods, by mistake of course, and shoot some hunter thinking he is an elk, or go fishing and fall in and drown, or get lost and the whole Forest Service has to look for them."

"What committee is this?" I asked Willard.

"Whatever it is," he said. "The Civic Club maybe, or I guess all of them put together. The same thing. Right now all these kids want to go out and ski. So what happens? The little brats break their leg. Two of them just last week, and I think that makes four already this season. A few get out of it easy, break a rib here and there, or their God damn arm. The way the committee sees it, and the way I have personally seen it for a long time, we have got to keep the kids away from these various influences and get a place to herd them into where you know where the hell they are at, out of trouble."

* The most ambitious country-for-the-kids program in New York is the Herald Tribune Fresh Air Fund, but the most interesting is that conducted in behalf of the Kips Bay Boys' Club. Kips Bay is an indentation of the East River just below the United Nations and adjacent to the old Gashouse District, famed in song, in story, and with respect to a St. Louis baseball team, circa 1930–35, starring Mr. Pepper Martin, third base. The idea here is to get these kids out fishing and camping and so on in strange and often distasteful surroundings, upstate. One day I noticed a can with a legend on it to this effect on the back bar of Hennessy's Bar & Grill, 978 Second Ave., Manhattan. I asked to see it and the bartender, Joe Reynolds, placed it on the bar and I donated twenty-five cents. I suggested to Joe that if he would keep the can on the bar itself he would get a much better response. He laughed in my teeth. "Put that on the bar," he said, "with all that money in it, and it would be gone out of here in ten minutes."

"Would the place have a bar in it?" I asked.

"That would be my dearest hope," he said. "It would save me a lot of work, chasing them out of here. But I guess not. Look, I'm not the Civic Club, or anything else. I just work here. I let them put the can on the bar. Why do you always have to ask so many questions? Every morning you come in here for your breakfast and I open the bottle and you say, 'Well, good morning, Willard. How are things?' Same old thing, and I get tired of it. Why don't you put a quarter in that can?"

"I would," I said, "if I thought they might use the money for another nice roller-skating rink, again."

Willard stopped wiping the bar and looked at me.

"Were you here then?" he asked.

"Yes," I said, "I lived here then . . ."

It was ten years before that, I think, I can't remember for sure; anyway it was winter, there was snow on the ground. Some committee or other, probably this same one, had put on a drive to build a roller-skating rink for the physical, mental, and moral benefit of all, with special emphasis on getting the adolescent slice of our society in out of the fresh air and other hazards.

This movement was a financial success and a large log structure was built beside the highway about a mile out of town. To introduce this torture chamber, which enthusiastically was endorsed by every registered endorsing agency in town, there was a Grand Opening, the purpose of which was to get together a crowd of Leading Citizens to show the younger or nonleading citizens how to approach the problems of life, or at least how to approach one of them.

Somebody sold my wife, Berry, two tickets on the basis of the fact that we had an adolescent son in residence in Jackson. This didn't impress me because our son, Sherwood, was the type of athlete to whom engagement in any sport is a form of suicide, and I told her to take them back and get a cash refund. But she pointed out that as a Leading Citizen I had a duty to perform, and never before having been called anything remotely resembling a Leading Citizen I sensed a chance to reverse my former standing and agreed not only to the tickets but to be present in person as an illustrious example of the American way of life.

I never had seen a roller-skating rink and of course never have seen one since. I thought I could just sit on a bench with the other patrons of the event and nod and smile benignly, somewhat after the manner of Archbishop Spellman reviewing the St. Patrick's Day parade in New York from the steps of St. Patrick's Cathedral. But I scarcely had sat down when I was approached in the matter of actually skating. The wife of one of Jackson's two doctors, an active leader in the roller-rink movement, brought the subject to my attention. She reminded me, with the support of Berry, which I certainly made a mental note of, that as a young man, in Minnesota, I used to play ice hockey. This unfortunately not only was true but had been a favorite conversational gem with me, including flourishes which I now regretted, whenever the subject of athletics came up in our circle, or whatever circle I found myself in.

In the end, some stockholder in St. John's Hospital, a famed Jackson institution, fastened a pair of roller skates to my shoes and I was told to stand up. I did, but this didn't last long. The next try was better and I rolled out onto the floor. Almost instantly I discovered the main difference between ice skating and roller skating. In ice skating you go at the same speed your skates do. In roller skating you do not. You go either faster or slower. Also, in ice skating, if you wish to make a turn, you simply make it; in roller skating you wait until you have come to a stop, then get out of the lady's lap and start off in a new direction. Now came the worst part, which I hate even to mention. In building a structure as large as that rink you cannot have cantilever construction, at least not with native materials, because the logs aren't long enough, so you must have pillars to hold up the roof. These were small, peeled, highly varnished logs, contributing to a type of architecture that does not fit in with roller skating, or anyway not with the type of roller skating I now was introducing to Wyoming.

When you hit slick poles of this sort and try to hang on, there is a tendency for the skates to go backward. (Unless, that is, you hit the pole backwards, in which case the skates go frontwards. Unlike ice skates, roller skates are radioactive and will not stand still even when that is all the skater wants out of life.) Suppose you are hugging one of these poles with all your might and main and the skates go backward, the tendency now is for your arms, and consequently the fore part of your body, to slide down to the floor, like a fireman answering a midnight alarm, taking the shock on your chin. This hurts, and on top of that splashes the audience with sweat, which is embarrassing. (I did not, however, have the bad luck that Bob Crisp had. Bob, a fine cowboy and one of the best rodeo riders extant, when he found himself sliding across the floor on his back, feet first, instinctively tried to fork one of these logs at a mile-a-minute clip and became the first hospital case.)

I tried to gather myself together, no mean trick, and really do something about my new standing in the community with whatever dignity I had left. My plan was simplicity itself: keep away from the poles, select only the trimmer laps to sit in, otherwise mind your own business. This would have worked out if the poles had kept their distance, but after a few more had wrapped their arms around me I bribed a juvenile delinquent to push me back to Berry, standing up.

Berry recognized me by my fingerprints, helped me into the car and drove me home, a distance I now estimated at ten miles. Upon putting me to bed she became quite concerned about my exclamations.

"Do you think I should call Doc?" she asked.

"No," I said, "by this time Doc will be too busy to pay any attention to poor little me. Doc sure hit the jackpot tonight. Why didn't you tell me his wife was chairman of the committee for the roller rink when you bought the tickets?"

"I don't think it's kind of you to talk like that," Berry said, with some feeling. "You know very well they had nothing like that in mind when they helped promote the rink. Doc has more practice than he can handle the way it is now."

"Of course I know it," I said. "Please stop crying."

"I'm glad you're not seriously hurt," she said, "and I'm sorry the evening wasn't pleasant."

"You can't have everything," I reminded her. "Being a Leading Citizen doesn't come for free."

It gives me unlimited joy to report that the rink was not a success. When the ultimate beneficiaries, as mentioned in the codicil, discovered that there was no bar attached, the sort of thing they could look ahead to eventually graduating into, they lost interest. No incentive. In an effort to keep the rink going, a second Adults' Night was proposed, but this fell flat (if I may be permitted a tender memory) when it was discovered there weren't any able-bodied adults left.

The hollow structure was taken down the following summer and the logs given back to the Indians. It was one of the easiest demolition jobs in all history, a circumstance in which I clearly had played a rather important part: my evening as a Leading Citizen had loosened it up to the point at which all the wreckers needed to take it the rest of the way down was a good strong breeze. In reckless assault I had hurled the living tissues of my body against this monster, never mind me, I was working for posterity itself, and in the end I flatter myself that I may have saved untold lives, including that of our son, Sherwood.

So now Willard and I resumed our conversation, which ended with my refusal to put a quarter into the can. Mr. Dews came in and greeted us both cordially, gracefully accepting an offer of a breakfast libation, on the house. He saw the can, with the slit in the top.

"What's that for?" he asked Willard.

Willard read the legend to him. "That's the place for your half dollar this morning, Dews," he said. "You'll never come closer to the jackpot."

Mr. Dews picked up the can and shook it, to be sure it was alive, then put it down. He sipped his drink and seemed lost in thought. Then he turned from the bar and stepped over to the bank of slot machines that faced it. He stopped before the 50-cent one, took a half dollar from his pocket and started to insert the coin. Before letting it go, he placed an arm against the machine and cradled his forehead with it.

"Let me think," he intoned. "I have two cans of crabmeat on my shelf, and one of lobster. Two Boston Brown Bread. Two beans, one salmon. Large-size salmon, by the way. Three sardine. I am enjoying a libation on the house; no charge. I have no rent to pay. I owe nobody. I haven't a worry in the world. I may as well——"

"Oh, for Christ sake drop it!" Willard called. "How often do I have to listen to your morning prayers? If you don't want to put it in the can here, for the kids, let go of it and have it over with."

Mr. Dews lifted his head. He looked back at the bar, and at the can standing upon it.

"Come on," Willard said. "Be a sport, Dews."

Mr. Dews hesitated.

"Didn't you ever have a kid of your own?" Willard asked, polishing a glass.

"How the hell do I know?" Mr. Dews said. He turned back to the machine and the half dollar clicked into it and gurgled a little and he closed his eyes as tightly as he could and pulled the lever. The machine sang its whirring song and the three symbols bounced to rest, one after the other, stopping in the places that the Mills Company, of Chicago, so far away, long had reserved for Mr. Dews.

chapter 11

The Great Snow-Statue Contest

THANKSGIVING safely stowed away, the blizzards began to sweep through in earnest and clogged the lifelines to the outside world almost to the point of suffocation—once fourteen snowslides ran on Teton Pass in a single day and twenty-two in Hoback Canyon—and Jackson Hole had to face up not only to this present inconvenience but to the possibility of full isolation, and for a matter of weeks: a possibility that soon was to become a fact.

The snow lay deep over the town, especially in the boxed-in square where swirling winds were most likely to drop their loads. When the merchants shoveled off their sidewalks, ramparts several feet high formed along the streets, the rhythmic scraping of the shovels playing an obbligato to the low swish of the persistent storms.

One relatively quiet but very cold afternoon John Deyo and Jack Francis, bartenders in the RJ, and George Lumley, proprietor of the drugstore next door, were resting on their shovels, disgusted with life, staring at this plethora of snow. Francis, intending only to make a casual remark, came up with something of practical value.

"Let's make a snow statue," he said.

Lumley, an artist at heart, picked up the idea. Why not? After all, the town now virtually was on its own, the social life had to go on without benefit of external influences; fun had to be had wherever it popped up, or could be made to pop up.

I was standing in the RJ Bar at the time, dining on a double rum and minding my own business, Mayor Harry Clissold also being present, when the three incipient sculptors came in from out front and explained their idea. All that remained to be resolved was the shape the statue should take. The mayor, a cynic born and bred, suggested that this was a detail that could be ignored, since no matter what they started out to make, in the end it would come out looking like everything else. In spite of this discouraging note a few ideas were discussed and discarded, then Lumley came up with the winner: a statue of a skier, a noble figure about to take off on God knew what intrepid adventure.

Sold.

The three artists, first refreshing themselves, now went off in various directions. Over a period of about an hour they returned, variously, with a piece of two-by-four long enough so that when it should be implanted in the snow it still would show about six feet, several pieces of lath, a zipper-front coverall such as those worn by filling-station attendants, some nails, a hammer, and a galvanized-iron bucket.

After warming their hands they got down to business. First they set up the two-by-four, then nailed two pieces of lath across this upright member about a foot from the top, forming a cross. They then draped the coveralls over this. It looked like hell, the most ghastly apparition possible to imagine. At this critical stage they came in to warm their hands again, leaving this awful caricature to flap slowly in the breeze, frightening passers-by almost to death, and no wonder.

Now they got to work. They filled the bucket with packed snow, then poured in enough beer to make a thick slush of it. (Beer makes better slush than water; it is just a little sticky. It also is cheaper, I believe, although I could be wrong here.) They took this outside and as Lumley shoved it into the top of the coveralls, at the neck, the others guided it down into the legs of the garment. This was repeated until something faintly resembling the nether extremities of an approximation of the human form began nearly to take shape. They now worked up, with bucketful after bucketful of this wonderful-smelling slush until, at long last, they seemed to have managed a fat misshapen scarecrow.

At this point I had to leave, it being time for my afternoon nap, and didn't get around until noon of the following day. The statue was finished, and it was startling. The skier stood there, glistening naked in the sun, his coveralls gone, his legs in the alert position of a person about to jump, and best of all he had a head on his shoulders. Briefly, a poem in white ice, dusted with just enough snow—or it may have been frost—so you couldn't see all the way through him.

He stood upon a pair of real skis (which, I was told, would be taken in at night) and held in one outthrust hand a ski pole (to be taken in at night), and his finely modeled head, featuring a square chin, was topped by an Alpine hat with a feather in it and he wore sunglasses (to be taken in at night).

They explained to me that the first thing that morning they had cut the coveralls away from the rock-hard frozen slush, chipped away parts of the body that didn't look right, added more slush where more was needed, gently fashioning it, then had made the head, freehand, and mounted it. After the new slush had frozen, which took only a few minutes, the entire statue was scraped and groomed with sharp knives, finally was doused with water, which instantly froze and gave a fine glacé finish to the job.

Everything was wonderful and we were standing at the window admiring the statue and watching people look at it as they passed, when word was given to us, by an incoming client, that there was mysterious activity in front of the Log Cabin, two doors down the street. Being a relatively uninterested party, I was sent out on patrol by Roy Jensen, at the cost to him of a hot rum. I found Roy Ransome, the head bartender, Jim Varley, a gambler, and an unidentified customer-in-residence placing on their rampart of snow something that looked like a rather large sawhorse, made of solid structural elements reinforced with lath.

I entered the Log Cabin, took a seat by the window, and ordered a hot rum, nonchalantly. It soon became clear that they were setting up some kind of animal, and when somebody presently showed up with a mounted deer head—which I learned later had been borrowed from the Elks' Club and in fact was the same one that had caused a certain misunderstanding there some time before—I figured out what kind of an animal it was to be; namely, a deer.

The workmen placed this deer head on a kind of special support at one of the sawhorse thing. The front end, I supposed. Now they began to plaster the frame with beer slush, the same as the RJ pioneers had used. They let each layer freeze before going on with the next, and while waiting for the layers to freeze they came in and had a hot rum. I also had one. Toward dusk they knocked off work and so did I, reporting back to the RJ that the Log Cabin chaps had come up with a new one, a two-headed deer, then went home.

The deer, which faced the skier, turned out fine. They had covered even the face and antlers with a fine coating of ice, powdered over with snow, and as a final touch had fastened a real deer tail to the opposite end of the lovely creature. This fluttered lightly in the breeze.

The next day—or maybe it was two days later, I was so tired I couldn't remember—Dudley Hayden, Jackson's leading plumber, a former National Park Ranger and at the moment president of the Jackson Civic Club (a post he later suddenly was to relinquish), happened to stroll past. A person of imagination and bounce, Dudley came up with something. Why not promote a snow-statue contest among the school children of the town? By this time they had learned the date of the Battle of Tours (A.D. 732), Christmas vacation was about to start, kids underfoot everywhere, time hanging heavy. Have them make these snowmen, or statues, in front of the business establishments, or in the park, facing them, for cash prizes to be put up by the merchants.

The proposal made an instant hit. No sooner said, that is to say, than done. Dudley collected $90 in cash and a lot of merchandise that the stores couldn't sell and got the enthusiastic backing of the School Board and the P-T.A. to say nothing of the fervent prayers of every mother of school-age children in town.

Rules were set up. This was to be strictly amateur and limited to kids up to and including the eighth grade. Assistance from older persons, in any way, was prohibited. The two professional statues then on view, the skier and the deer, were not to count and were not to be copied, except with respect to the technique—excluding the beer—that had been used. A panel of judges was set up, this to consist of Mrs. Dick Reimers, a housewife; Gladys Smith (no relation to Mary Pickford), wife of the barber; Conrad Schwiering, an artist, and Gordon Guffey, Superintendent of Schools. Dudley himself, ex officio, was to vote only in case of a tie.

The kids were let loose and they started to work on half a dozen projects, but it quickly became apparent that the older and infinitely wiser generation couldn't keep its mitts off what the young people had in mind doing, here as elsewhere. At that time the kids were fond of catching onto the rear of a car and sliding along behind it for half a block

Chicken
BAR
CAFE
Chicken
Steak
Steak Trout
COCKTAILS
BAR
Trout
Silver Spur
MERRY CHRISTMAS

or so, using their overshoes as skis, and all the Browning Study Clubs in town were against it (members of the clubs were too old to do it without falling on one or another of their bulges). As a consequence of this, the first snow statue to emerge was that of a little boy with one arm in a sling, supporting with his other arm a sign, not painted by any amateur, that read I WILL NOT HITCH ON BEHIND AUTOMOBILES.

This just about stopped the whole program; you can't kid kids, of all people: they know when they are being taken for a ride, and this deal looked very much like another one of those things. (They also instinctively knew, perhaps, that there was no practical way of making a snow statue showing a car being driven on the highway at seventy miles an hour by the older and wiser generation and hitting a telephone pole, instantly killing all five occupants.)

The kids quit work but were brought back into the fold by professional mediators. One of the first things they completed, to the astonishment of the citizenry, was a Blue Ox. This plainly was supposed to be a replica of the famous Blue Ox, friend and companion of that legendary lumberjack, Paul Bunyan, a subject about as far removed from the date of the Battle of Tours as any reasonable person could imagine.*

The youngsters were at a disadvantage because they never had seen a real ox of any color, and the shape of the animal was not all that the P-T.A. could have desired, but the sculptors made up for this by making it really blue, not only on

* Please excuse me for repeatedly bringing up the date of the Battle of Tours. One bitter cold day in midwinter when I was riding a horse through Jackson Hole I stopped in at a little log schoolhouse to get warm, and the teacher, a handsome babe if I ever saw one, was asking one of the pupils that very question. At recess I asked her if her wards knew anything about the history and the background, the geological formations, the whole reason-for-being, of Jackson Hole. Even the heathen coyote tells her puppies what the local score is as soon as their eyes are open. She said no, this was not called for by the curriculum, but the date of the Battle of Tours definitely was listed by the Wyoming Department of Education.

the surface but all the way through: the little geniuses simply had mixed bluing with their snow and ice. Proving that art is nobody's baby, but is found where you find it.

A few minor figures came up here and there and one whole grade-school class, with the obvious approval of influential persons, pooled their manpower and put up a huge snowman, fourteen feet high, in the middle of the park. It plainly was Santa Claus, and was supposed to blast its way to first prize through sheer size and an overwhelming spiritual, or anyway seasonal, approach. But in the final reckoning the indomitable individuality and resourcefulness and imagination of Jackson Hole showed its hand even in the halls of adolescent education. Some of the smaller and sharper boys worked up a statue that was not only heroic in concept but amazingly accurate in execution. They got to work at a spot in the park just across the street from the Cowboy Bar, which in itself proved that they knew which side their snow was buttered on: the RJ and the Log Cabin had been pre-empted, and the Silver Dollar, a half block off the town square, was out of the running. Following the know-how, as it is called, of the RJ crowd, they got hold of an old pair of levis, small size, faded and bowlegged, hung them on a frame, and filled them with wet snow.*

* Levi Strauss, manufacturer of Western clothing, is one of the few industrialists in the United States whose foremost product, in this case trousers, or pants, made of blue denim and copper-riveted for strength, has added what amounts to a generic term to the American language. Everybody knows what "levis" are. They make their wearers appear to be bowlegged, but this is an optical illusion. Cowboys are no more bowlegged than you are. They look that way because their levis, which are cut perfectly straight, after a few wettings and a few dryings follow the curvature of a horse's belly. There are fewer bowlegged cowboys than there are, say, insurance salesmen. Bowleggedness is caused by a youngster's trying to walk while his bones still are soft. A cowboy, as a rule, has sat on a horse since he was a week old. Some of them reach the age of seventy before finding out what their legs are for. And Levi Strauss, by the way, never wrote any music, although it is hard to convince a true Westerner of that. You might as well try to tell him that one of fiction's foremost characters, a hypnotist, was not a person by the name of Slim Galli.

Above this they managed a torso, I don't know how, and a round head topped by an old Stetson hat (not worth bringing in at night). Reversing the process used at the RJ, they covered the torso with a red cotton shirt, and left the levis where they were. This plainly was a cowboy. Following the stance of the skier, he, too, had a hand outstretched before him, at arm's length. But instead of a ski pole the hand held a brown bottle of Schlitz beer. Beneath this ensemble rested a sign—amateur in execution—that read MERRY CHRISTMAS!

Nobody else had thought of MERRY CHRISTMAS!

The fact that when it was time for the jury, or panel, to walk around the square and do the judging, somebody removed the bottle of beer from the hand of the cowboy and substituted, temporarily, a cedar wreath tied with a huge bow of pink ribbon may have had something to do with the cowboy taking first prize. In any case it did take first prize, Dudley breaking a tie vote.

The Santa Claus got second prize, virtually by default, and to the delight of all the Blue Ox got third. There were several consolation prizes, but to the cheers of the younger element in the populace the boy with the broken arm didn't even get Honorable Mention.

The next day, with the bottle back in the hand of the cowboy, the inevitable reaction set in and things began to get a little rough. The people of Jackson always are choosing up sides about something or other, and now it was about the cowboy getting first prize.

This was considered a moral error, and steps were taken to deny him his honors. But a good many people were found who had the courage to stand up for him, even a few stray Republicans. It was pointed out that the prizes were supposed to be awarded on the basis of juvenile imagination and artistic accomplishment, not on that of any Message, as exemplified in the boy with the broken arm. As to the beer—

and this was an empty bottle, as I found to my disgust late one dark night during a period of financial depression—the little boys simply were interpreting Nature as they had observed it around them, a high and noble function of the true artist, and if the opposition wanted a change, let them change Nature.

The anti-cowboy crowd pointed out that the cowboy plainly was on a bender. The pro-bender people said okay, what of it, he probably was due for one, and who was responsible for the culture and prosperity of Jackson Hole, Santa Claus? The dispute died out when Dudley Hayden, who had been pegged as casting the deciding vote, resigned as president of the Civic Club.

The big surprise of the rhubarb was Mayor Clissold, who inexplicably and to the amazement of everybody had sided with the anti-cowboy element, but this was cleared up when he explained that he was not against the statue, or the idea, as such, but that as Teton County distributor for Anheuser-Busch, Inc., of St. Louis, makers of Budweiser beer, giving first prize to a statue involving a bottle of Schlitz had embarrassed him professionally.

So the snow-statue contest was over, but some of the statues themselves lingered on, well into the February thaw. During their brief stay among us, their lives were not without incident. Some vandal decorated the skier—whose pectoral muscles in the first place were considered by thoughtful persons to be too large for a male athlete—with two halves of grapefruit and two cherries, all frozen snugly in place. This caused a municipal furor; even after the fruit was removed the yellow stains were with the skier for the rest of his little life.

The big buck deer, while he lived, lived life to the hilt. One night Slim Linville reported that four deer, all of them does, had bedded down in the park. This was during a time of bright moonlight, and the place selected by the does was directly across the street from the lovely buck. They left town by day but returned, in decreasing numbers, every night. The original four dropped to three, then to just two, and finally only one was left. This one was faithful to the end, a lithesome creature with soulful eyes, deep and limpid even in the moonlight.

With the first touch of thaw, however, the big buck's head came loose. First it sagged, then one mild day, just at high noon, it dropped off, and the little doe left town forever.

During his lonely night patrols, especially when the moon was out, Slim had developed a latent streak of deep sentiment in his nature, and the conclusion of this romance hurt him to the quick. "It was the same old story," he said, "of the country girl and the glamor of city life. But who can blame her? I tell you, there were times, when the moon was especially bright, that the big buck seemed alive. The moon put glints in him that you don't see in an ordinary deer. It was eerie. I wouldn't be at all surprised if that buck had taken a few trips over into the park. Some people don't believe me when I tell about that last doe. But I saw her, night after night. Why, I damn near wept when that buck's head dropped off."

It pains me to have to say that the cowboy came to no good end. When his creators filled the levis with the wet snow they didn't put in any lath or other bones, and right after the contest the cowboy began to get bowleggeder and bowleggeder, until from the waist down he looked like a doughnut. To make it worse, one leg, the left one, began to bow worse than the other, causing him to list, gradually more and more, and at the same time some sort of vitamin deficiency made him lean a little forward.

The end came with those midwinter chinook zephyrs that were the undoing of the big buck deer, and that caused the skier, by the way, to slide down his last long hill, slaloming gracefully into the street, where he rudely was cut in two by a passing truck.

The cowboy's hand lost its grip and he dropped his bottle of beer into the snow, then heeled over pitifully. A quick change in the weather almost saved him, but it was too late. He sank to eternal rest, one leg and one arm gallantly aloft to the end, a captain going down with his ship: an object lesson in arrested motion until the snows finally drifted over him and he passed into history. Gone, as the obituaries say, but not forgotten.

I am sorry to have to close this chapter on such a mournful note. I had hoped to keep it cheerful, and I tried, but the facts of life—especially when this snow-statue life, at best a transient thing, is conceived in rigor mortis to start with—were too much for me.

chapter 12

A Pleasant Libation

As Christmas moved in apace, everybody busy at one thing or another, I was invited one day by Mr. Dews to pay him a holiday visit in his apartment beneath the Silver Dollar Bar. I had met Mr. Dews some years before, when he first came to Jackson Hole, but I knew him better now, had been a guest in his quarters a few times, and we had enjoyed a few libations at the bar, especially for breakfast.

I was standing at the bar alone one forenoon breaking my fast with a bottle of beer and passing the time of day with Willard Miner when a man came in with a large bucket filled with ice cubes, which he dumped into an underbar bin. He then went out to a truck parked in the street and returned with another bucketful, and upon emptying this bucket he accepted a quick one on the house and gave Willard a slip to sign. Willard signed it and the man went away. I asked Willard what he had to pay for the ice and he said $1.75 for two buckets.

"With ten billion tons of ice within walking distance of here," somebody behind me said, "it costs four cents a pound at the bar. At that rate——"

I looked over my shoulder and there was Mr. Dews, up betimes this morning, and pert. I asked him to join me at my morning meal. He accepted. "A modest libation," he said, "is ever welcome." He chose whiskey and directed Willard to put two ice cubes in his water chaser. "As I was saying,"

Mr. Dews continued, "at the rate they pay for ice cubes around here, if you slip while crossing the street and bump yourself on a tender spot you can console yourself with the thought that you are sitting on a hundred dollars or so worth of good ice. You couldn't do better than that in the Klondike, on an informal basis, if you were looking for gold."

"It's a question of the shape of the ice, Dews," Willard said impatiently, "and you know that damned well. And another thing, what would you do for ice cubes in summer if you didn't keep Harry busy in the winter?"

"Then what does Willard do next?" Mr. Dews asked me rhetorically, ignoring Willard. "The place here gets chilly and he checks the fuel oil and it's low so he phones to Idaho Falls, at great expense, and a guy drives an oil tanker a couple hundred miles and risks his neck crossing Teton Pass so Willard can get the bar warm enough to melt the ice cubes he has bought."

"Oh, for Christ sake!" Willard said. He walked up to the other end of the bar and rolled a cigarette.

"You're up early," I said to Mr. Dews.

"My day off. I like to get up early on my day off. No sense in sleeping on your own time." He tossed off his drink, drank part of his chaser, rattled the ice cubes and placed the glass firmly on the bar. "Suppose we repair to my apartment downstairs," he suggested, "and enjoy a further Christmas libation, as my guest. I see enough of this bar professionally."

I agreed to this and we left, passing Willard, who was pretending to read a newspaper, and went down the stairs and into the basement. Mr. Dews led the way to his quarters, which were formed, as I have mentioned, by walling off a corner of the basement with stacks of beer cases reaching almost to the ceiling. There was an opening between the Coors and the Pabst, and Mr. Dews, slight in stature and slender in width, deftly slipped through. I made it with a bit more effort. He found the droplight and turned on the electric bulb. "Your door is getting narrower," I said.

He glanced at my waist.

"I believe it is," he said. "I piled the last shipment of Coors a little closer to the Pabst. I find this keeps out a certain number of people. I like guests, but I don't like them too fat. Show me a man with a belly big enough so he can't get through that opening and I'll show you a man who has got something on his mind that will not work out to your advantage. I don't know why it is. Sit down on the bed, there."

I sat on an iron cot, something like a hospital bed only lower, neatly made up with an Army blanket for a cover. At one side of the bed was a board, somehow fastened to the concrete wall, that served as a shelf. Upon it were some toilet articles, a tin basin, and so on. At one end of it were a considerable number of small cans containing lobster, crabmeat, salmon, shrimp, Boston Brown Bread, sardines, and other tinned food, with seafood heavily favored, especially crab.*

Above the board was a small mirror, and standing at one side was Mr. Dews's wardrobe, a box about seven feet high, with a curtain across the front of it. I had seen this before, it was an ordinary coffin box used for shipping bodies out to the railroad. Mr. Dews had scrounged it from the hardware store, but the curtain, startlingly rich, almost like cloth-of-gold, was new.

"You have a new curtain," I said.

Mr. Dews nodded. "Picked it up in a casual way when they were redecorating the cocktail lounge." He looked around his apartment. "Yes, I have a nice place here. I keep

* It reliably is reported (Miner) that when news of the Japanese attack on Pearl Harbor, December 7, 1941, with war certain, came to Jackson and was relayed to Mr. Dews, he blinked his eyes a couple of times and said, "Good God! If this is true, it means no more Japanese crab!" I don't know where Mr. Dews got his exotic supplies, but he always had them on hand in his apartment.

fixing it up, little by little. Everything I want or need." He glanced up at the ceiling, across which ran several pipes. "Central heating, as they say in England, and when I wish to bathe there's always an empty room upstairs, or at least one where the people are out for a horseback ride." He snapped his fingers. "Well, well, well! First things first!" He went to his north wall and extracted a hunting knife from between two of the cases, then turned to me. "Schlitz, Coors, Ranier, Acme, Pabst, Sheridan, Budweiser—just name it."

I chose Bud, for which Mr. Dews had to turn to his east wall. Getting down on his knees he carefully cut through a strip of paper tape along the side of a case near the floor, opened the carton, and brought out four bottles. He quickly uncapped two with an opener he had in his pocket and handed me one. "Not quite as cold as it is upstairs," he said, "but it keeps very cool, down there next to the floor. I never drank much beer, myself, until I came to work at the Silver Dollar, here, and they gave me this apartment." He sat down on a box. "Now to resume our conversation. Take that thing about the ice cubes. The same thing goes on in other directions. Like snow and the Christmas trees. Last year I was invited out to a Christmas party. I seldom ever get invited out and when I am invited out I a damn sight seldomer go. The hell with it. But this time it was a lady who was spending her first winter here in Jackson, she was from the East and took a liking to it, or maybe didn't have carfare home, but however it was she rented herself a nice little house out at the edge of town and wanted to be a part of us, so I decided to go on out."

Mr. Dews drank some of his beer and I drank some of mine and he asked me if it was cold enough and I told him it was just right and he continued:

"As it turned out we had quite a storm, and on Christmas

Eve the snow was deep, and still falling. I had to walk a mile up the road. This was all right because the plow had been through, but the house was a good thirty feet from the road and the plow had piled up the snow and it looked like I was the first one to arrive—a good idea when it comes to cocktail parties, if you can do it without making too much of a noticeable point of it—and I didn't know what to do but finally I just bucked into that snow with all my might, and knifed through, which I can do on account of my build, if it isn't too far.

"When I finally got into the house I had snow packed up inside my pants and the tops of my overshoes were jammed full and to tell the truth I had snow all over me. My hostess got a shovel and a broom and it took us a good five minutes to get me free of the snow, I almost had to undress, and after we had shoveled the snow outdoors she offered me a libation, which I took charge of. She seemed quite nervous and I found she was worrying about her Christmas tree. She had an artistic nature and she didn't want her tree, which was standing in a corner of the room, to have too many ornaments on it. It didn't have very many, along with some Christmas cards she had tied to it. 'I wanted it to fit into the country,' she said. 'I wanted it to look natural, with lots of snow. I sent to Salt Lake for some artificial snow, but it didn't come, and I tried to find some cotton batting here in town to put around the base and the lower branches, but they didn't have a thing. I'm terribly disappointed. What shall I do?' "

Mr. Dews finished his beer and I finished mine and he opened two more.

"She even had tried to get some popcorn, to string or to pile around the tree," Mr. Dew continued, "but there had been a strong run on popcorn and the stores were out of it. I suggested to her that there was a little actual snow outside; in other words, I asked her if she wanted some snow why in

Christ's name didn't she use some snow. She said it didn't look enough like snow, it didn't sparkle. And besides that it would make a mess. I told her to put some papers on the floor, and when her guests came in just put the snow they would be covered with under the tree and on it, and she would be all fixed. She accepted the idea. And her tree, I don't care if you believe it, had been shipped in from Idaho Falls. Most of the trees here are shipped in from Idaho Falls. At the latest count there were sixteen billion, three hundred million, seven hundred and forty thousand, a hundred and eighty-nine Christmas trees growing here in Jackson Hole. I counted them myself. But you can't go out and get one. The snow's too deep, and if it's on National Forest land you have to get a permit—from Washington, for all I know—and in the end it's cheaper to buy an imported tree, bring it in over Teton Pass. Just like the ice cubes."

We enjoyed the rest of our beer and Mr. Dews cut open a new case. "Mind having Pabst?" he said. "I don't like to take too many out of any one case, on account of inventory, although they won't be getting to these bottom cases for years. I'll see to that."

I said anything was okay. "What are you going to do on your day off?" I asked. "I mean today, by way of celebration."

Mr. Dews opened the case and opened the beers.

"Well . . . I plan on getting dressed and taking a stroll around the square. Then I think I'll go over to the Open Range Café, Jack Moore's place, and have me a quiet meal. A good thick steak, never mind the cost. Take my time. You know, I haven't walked around the square since last summer. It was quite an experience. I stopped in at the Cowboy to see the show, and I was surprised. They had a ventriloquist there. I can take a ventriloquist or leave him alone, but this one was a kind I never saw before. He had two dummies, one on each knee, and the three of them carried on a conversation even when the fellow was looking the other way, and even when he was making some remarks to the audience on the side. Then he sang *We Were Sailing Along on Moonlight Bay* in four voices all at once, taking the part of a quartet. The damn thing was quite touching, took me back many years, but he did it. And they had a fan dancer there, the best I ever saw, although I may also say she was the first I ever saw."

"Flo Ash," I said.

"A beautiful girl," Mr. Dews said.

"She gave me her liver just before she left for Las Vegas a few weeks ago," I said.

Mr. Dews put down his bottle and looked at me. "I beg your pardon?" he said.

"She had an elk liver," I explained. "A hunter gave it to her, and she left it over at Bob McGee's lunch counter to be put in the refrigerator. She hadn't time to eat it before she left and she came around to me and said she understood I was on shorts and she had the elk liver and it was all mine. She called up Charlotte Simons and told her to give it to me, and Charlotte cooked it. It was wonderful."

Mr. Dews lifted his bottle in a salute to life. "That's the way it is," he said. "One day it's good and the next day it's bad. So everybody takes care of everybody else. Getting back to last summer, when I took my walk around the square. I had on a nice suit, my Panama hat, and my gold tie pin. I seldom get out. I haven't even seen the snow statues they tell me about. They got this skier and a deer and a cowboy and so on. Santa Claus, and so forth. All I know is the cowboy got first prize and some people were arguing about it, upstairs. Nobody is ever satisfied."

Mr. Dews got up from the box on which he had been sitting and went to his shelf and picked up something and brought it to me. "My tie pin," he said. "A gold dollar. A very rare thing. I've been offered up to fifteen dollars for it. I just laugh at them. I brought it out from Baltimore many years ago. My mother gave it to me."

As Mr. Dews put it back on the shelf I noticed something I hadn't seen before, a piece of string stretched between the shelf and the wardrobe, from which hung a number of pieces of thread, each with a needle attached to it.

"What the hell is that?" I asked.

"Oh . . . needles and thread," Mr. Dews said. "The way it is, I don't see very well any more, of late years. I can get around all right, but no fine work. I can read a little, if I get my face close enough to the paper, but I can't thread a needle. I always like to keep my own clothes in repair. I was taught years ago, and I know how. Anything needs sewing, a button on my topcoat or a shirt, a little tear, whatever it is, I do it myself. It's the way I was brought up. But as I say I can't thread a needle so I buy a dollar's worth at a time and a spool or two of thread, different kinds, and a friend of mine threads all the needles for me and hangs them up here."

"That's certainly nice," I said. "Who does it for you?"

Mr. Dews cleared his throat. "Willard. He's handy at things like that. He helps me out in a number of ways. The only thing I got against Willard is the way he hits the ceiling of my apartment, here, with his baseball bat, every time the Yankees win. My God, I don't care if the Yankees win, just so it's not the World Series against the Dodgers. Let them go ahead and win, Willard doesn't have to wake me up about it all summer when I work nearly all night and need a little sleep. Does he hit the floor of the bar when the Dodgers win? Of course not; what does he care about the Dodgers? Well, Willard has his own ways, and he's set about it. But however it is he threads my needles for me, and we get along fine."

chapter 13

Christmas in a Christmas Card

JUST at the foot of the Grand Tetons, at the edge of a dense forest of lodgepole pine and spruce, nestle the headquarters of Grand Teton National Park. This complex consists of an administration building, with a garage and other accessory structures, and several houses, in which live the Park Service personnel. These houses, which are Alpine in architecture and very attractive, are scattered around among the trees. In winter they look as though they had been lifted out of one of those old-fashioned Christmas cards showing sharply peaked buildings, heavily capped with snow upon which sparkling mica had been sprinkled, to the disgust of the Post Office Department.

The Park is about twenty miles north of Jackson, higher in altitude, and the snow is much deeper; often, in order to enter a house, you have to walk down or even climb down to the door, and in some of the administration offices the lights are kept on all day because the snow is higher than the windows at times. The people do not get around much, once winter sets in—although you can count on them for the cocktail hour in Jackson—because it's such a chore to get out, and might be an even worse one getting back. The group is a congenial one, self-sufficient, and special occasions and holidays provide welcome interludes and are given the works.

I was invited to spend a couple of days with Sunny and

Esther Allan at Headquarters just before Christmas, and it was wonderful up there. I fed suet to the Canada jays that came to the kitchen window sill, and Esther made heaps of sourdough pancakes. We visited neighbors, and the whole thing was very pleasant. The main topic of conversation, I found, was the impending Christmas Eve party, a community celebration to be held at the home of Chief Ranger Paul Judge and his wife, Frances. The women were making all the various things that women make at a time like that: pies and cakes and other poisonous confections, and decorating the Judges' house, the kids stringing popcorn for the Christmas tree, presents being wrapped and hidden in closets, and so on and so forth.

The high point of the evening was to be the arrival of Santa Claus, in the person of Sunny Allan. His was to be no ordinary entrance. He was to come in on snowshoes, preceded by three other rangers with Army blankets over their shoulders and branches of spruce held at either side of their heads to simulate the horns of the reindeer they were supposed to represent. They were to be attached to each other, and to Sunny, by a rope. They would come into the house by way of the kitchen, trot into the large main room, sweep halfway around it with a flourish, then the reindeer would stand aside, exposing Santa with his arm upraised, his belly shaking with laughter, triumphant.

However, they made two mistakes in their planning.

First, they decided, at the last moment, to fasten roller skates under Sunny's snowshoes. This would allow him to come in effortlessly, in style, just as though standing in a sleigh. The other mistake was in their failure to think of this fancy touch, and tell me about it, before I departed for Jackson.

The roller skates were left over from the adventure of

the roller rink years before. Most of the skaters, when the rink came to its sad end, had donated their skates to the Baptist church—as soon as they got out of the hospital—for some kind of rummage sale, and Sunny, who has streaks of absent-mindedness, thoughtlessly had bought a pair. He had stowed them away in some shed or attic and just now had come across them.

I didn't hear about this development of the plan until early Christmas Eve, when a game warden, who had stopped in at the Park on his way down from up-country, mentioned the extra surprise that Sunny was going to spring on the womenfolk and the kids; namely, coming in with roller skates fastened to his snowshoes.

The full impact of this bit of casual news didn't hit me until a minute later. When it did, a kind of a dull pain swept me; my abdomen became a vacuum; I closed my eyes in horror as the impending nightmare flashed, or rather zigzagged, through my aching mind . . .

There stands the tree, the beautiful tree, with the presents arranged beneath it. At one end of the room a long auxiliary table, made of planks laid on sawhorses, has been set up, and here is a six-quart pot of steaming coffee, a great bowl of Tom & Jerry, and a buffet-style layout of the food the women lovingly had prepared for this Christmas Eve feast.

Everything is ready, the moment is at hand . . .

Hush! Hark! Is that the rattle of a cowbell, just outside the house? Whose jolly voice is that, calling out the names of Dunder and Blitzen and Dancer and Prancer and the rest?

The door swings open, the reindeer dash in, pulling Santa on his roller-skate-equipped snowshoes! The graceful animals half circle the room, then swerve aside as Santa, belly shaking with happy holiday laughter, is catapulted——

Why, oh why, hadn't they told me of their plans? Why was I, the foremost roller-skating expert of Wyoming, not asked what was bound to happen next?

Santa cannot make the turn! Santa cannot stop! The damned skates carry him straight on, at maddening speed, straight at the table, straight into the jaws of chaos itself——

The table breaks up in the slow motion of inescapable collision, like the ice going out of the Yukon in the spring, as depicted by Walt Disney. A stack of plates float to the floor and gradually disintegrate . . . The coffee lifts itself into the air, hovers over the scene, spreads itself languidly, then descends in a graceful arc and caresses the cake, which, picking up the tempo, unfolds like the petals of a morning-glory greeting the dawn . . . The Tom & Jerry flows, lavalike, across the floor and into the presents beneath the tree, leaving this wonderful drink unfit for human consumption, a devastating thought, a calamity . . . Santa is sitting on a platter of turkey, his face covered with mince pie . . . From the distance comes the slow moaning wail of a child . . .

But enough of this! I came out of my trance, and sprang to action. The telephone! I dashed to it, and after an excruciating delay managed to get through to the Judge home. Frances answered. She seemed breathless, disturbed.

"Frances!" I cried. "Don't let Sunny put those roller skates under his snowshoes! Stop him! Please . . ."

But I was too late.

Part 3. THE LONG PULL

chapter 14

"She's Here"

A LONE, lorn cowboy came in out of the cold noon and stepped up to the RJ bar and rested his elbow upon it. He nodded, if a bit weakly, to Roy Jensen.*

"Give me a hot one, Roy," he said.

"You mean you're off the green stuff?" Roy asked.

"Oh, hell, it's another year." The cowboy looked out the window at the statue of the skier. (Although, as I have mentioned, all the statues were to come to sad ends during the February thaw, they still were in full bloom at the year's end.) "She's sure here, Roy."

"She sure as hell is. Stick of cinnamon in the hot one?"

"Yes." The cowboy counted on his fingers. "January, February, April, March."

"March, then April. And don't forget May."

"That's right. I forgot May. January, February, April . . . I mean January, February, March, April, *May*. Firewood, feed lots, calving, and back to the hills."

* On November 8, 1955, Roy was elected president of the National Licensed Beverage Association of America at their convention in Chicago. He was the first person from west of the Mississippi ever to be elected to this office.

"Or back to the Crème de Menthe," Roy suggested.

The cowboy grinned. "Well . . . maybe it could be, at that. I might go back with a dude outfit again. I don't know. They're a nuisance, but still on the other hand . . ." He sipped the drink that Roy now placed before him. "How cold is she out out today?"

"Ten, twelve, fifteen below." Roy pushed the cowboy's money back to him. "Happy New Year."

* * *

So it's New Year's Day.

Few of the townspeople are in the bars. They had it last night, and now, in blessed retreat to the pleasant shelter of the fireside, relaxation comes like a warm bath, leisurely enjoyed in release from the climactic activities of the year-end holidays.

But for the cocktail-hour guests from up-country and down-country and all around the Hole it is a sad day, a sad time; they walk the sidewalks slowly in the cold, the hard snow crunching under their boots, squeaking and whining, or stop in at the bars for a hot one, as the lone, lorn cowboy had done.

When the cowboy said, "She's here," he hadn't meant the snow and the cold, for both were on hand as early as October, nor did he mean winter, as such, for winter long since had begun.

In the spoken and unspoken language of Jackson Hole he merely meant that the Long Pull was at hand.

This is the time between the theoretical end of the cocktail hour at the holiday season—this termination, as I have suggested, being subject to an extremely loose interpretation —and the arrival of that bit of heaven known locally as May. Then, or thereabouts, give or take a couple of weeks one way or the other, the movement of people and of animals will reverse that of last fall: cowboys and cows * and elk and deer to high pastures, the dude wranglers and rangers and game wardens and others to battle stations, then the incoming beautiful cocktail waitresses and lovely lady shills (the coyotes by this time having retreated), and the summer gamblers and other concessionaires, then finally the first tourist, the first dude girl, and the first arrow to be plucked from the heart of Cock Robin (also known as Slim).

Meantime, there is more to plow through than just the deep snow, which, although hard to handle, can't talk back. The dark days of cabin fever—that scourge of the sequestered, when distorted imaginations take over and lifelong friends forget to nod to each other, and a bitter communal loneliness settles over the valley—lie not too far ahead.

The Long Pull? Yea, in all directions, up and down and sideways and on into the fourth dimension.

* * *

One afternoon in January I was on my way to the post office when a car pulled up beside me and Pat Patterson rolled the window down and leaned out.

"Let's go up and look at the Tetons," he said.

This seemed a sound idea, so I got in.

Because of a long butte that borders Jackson on the west you can't see the great peaks from town, you have to drive up-country three or four miles and there the Tetons rise before you, fifteen miles away but as close to you as your hand. This dramatic outcropping of the earth's crust, or what-

* "Cows" is a generic term in the West. Girl calves are heifers, boy calves, after emasculation, become steers, a cow is a big girl who has had a baby, and a bull is a bull. Heifers supply most of our veal, steers supply all of our fine steaks and roasts, cows—other than dairy cows, which furnish babies of all ages and kinds with a tasteless and nauseous lacteal fluid—supply cheap meat of questionable quality, and bulls make the finest hamburger meat there is: the toughness taken care of by grinding, the flavor still the best of all. To save time, all domestic cattle are called "cows" in the West.

ever it is, exerts an influence on local people that is deeper and longer-lasting than the ephemeral impact on the passers-by. More and more tourists, it seems to me, want to see the West—and in fact all of life itself—in a dimension of 2¼″ by 2¼″, or some other little square or rectangle. They stop their cars, tires screeching perhaps, jump out and ask each other, with visible agitation, "Shall I give it f.16 and 50, or do you think f.22 and 25?" Whatever they are worried about, they want to take a million acres home in their vest pocket.

In Jackson Hole, the vest pocket is obsolete. The people who live here take the Tetons and all the other mountains in stride, deeply, and forever. They do not pretend to understand them or even to know them. Once I asked a man—his name was Charlie Hedrick—who had homesteaded in the Hole and now was close to eighty years old, "Don't you ever get tired looking at those same mountains?"

He looked at me curiously. "Those mountains are never the same," he said.

So Pat and I drove up toward the Tetons. Winter driving here in the valley is something of a trick. In this modern age they have a rotary plow, and this thing cuts a snow canyon the walls of which often are higher than the cars, and at night when everything is white in your headlights, and you have no idea where the turns are, you have to feel your way, which can be irritating at fifty or sixty miles an hour. You hit the snow wall and have to back up and start all over again, which is a waste of time. Even in daylight, everything dazzling, you travel more or less by compass.

"It's going to be a tight winter, Pat," I said.

"Let it be," Pat said, skidding lightly into a six-foot wall of snow and bouncing off. "I like winter to be winter and snow to be snow. Last winter I went down to Arkansas to visit some relatives, and what I'm going to tell you is the damn truth, so help me, as sure as I'm sitting here. One night I was invited to a party, few tables of cards. When it came midnight, time to go home—they close up early down there—the first couple to leave went out to their car and they came running back in and they were frightened to death.

" 'We're snowed in!' they said, ready to cry.

"I didn't know anything about any snow but they called up the highway department to see when the roads would be open, and our host began to see what food supplies he had on hand for the emergency, I'm a son of a bitch if he didn't. Finally I went outside, and what the hell do you think I found? One inch of snow. In some places, no snow at all. Strike me dead if I'm telling a lie. When I said I was going to get in my car and drive on to my hotel, you would think I was Admiral What's-his-name going on another expedition to the South Pole. So help me God. I never saw anything like it. I told them that up in Jackson Hole we didn't even *use* the snow until it was two years old."

We came to the end of the butte and there was a place where the wind had swept the snow away and Pat pulled over and stopped the car and we smoked a cigarette and looked at the Tetons. "Seventh wonder of the world," Pat said. After a while we started the engine and turned the car around and we went back to Jackson.

I had forgotten to mail my letters, and anyway I had some other work to do, so it was about four o'clock the next morning when I went over to the post office again. It was a calm time, the moon shining down on the snow, giving it life, and the coyotes were singing louder than ever in the hills, the cold thin air bringing it in, and after I had gone to the post office I decided to take a little walk around the square.

Then I heard somebody else walking, and from the slow cadence I knew it was Slim Linville, so I stood still until

I spotted him, just passing Lumley's drugstore, taking it easy. I went over and met him.

I told him I had been up to see the Tetons with Pat Patterson, and we talked a while, quietly. You don't talk loud when nothing else is loud.

The statue of the skier was just beside us. "You know," Slim said, "I'm supposed to be the one that put those grapefruit on the front of the skier."

"You didn't," I said.

"I know it," Slim said. "But I was on patrol that night and I watched. You know that. It must have been thirty below."

"It was plenty cold," I said, inadvertently glancing at my hands. "If anybody wants to make an issue about your doing it, tell me."

"It's all over," Slim said. He nodded toward the buck deer, a noble figure in the moonlight. "You know, there's a pretty little doe comes in nearly every night and settles down in the park, across the street, and just looks and looks at that buck. You ought to see her eyes. She——"

"Slim, you told me," I said.

Slim waited a minute. "You probably don't believe it," he said.

"We all believe it, Slim," I said quietly. "We've believed it right along."

"I guess so," Slim said. "Please excuse me. You know how it is, you walk around here all night, and it's one of those things that gets on your mind. At this time of year, especially. I don't mean to keep mentioning it." He laughed a little. "Maybe you can have cabin fever even if you don't live in one."

We stood there a while and listened to the coyotes in the hills, in the distance, wherever they were, then we said good night and Slim continued his slow walk and I went on home to my cabin and to bed.

chapter 15

The Dry Cold

ACCORDING to established legend the cold at the altitude of Jackson Hole, which runs about 7,000 feet at the valley floor and goes on up to 14,000 at the top of the Grand Teton, is so thin and dry that you scarcely notice it; it's as sweet and harmless as a little teeny-weeny kitten. In the area of immediate personal comfort this theory, under Chamber of Commerce pressure, is acceptable, up to a point, but it also is dangerous. You can feel so warm and comfortable, in fifty below, thankful you don't live in New York, where the cold is damp, that you are likely to forget that you are freezing to death, perhaps so suddenly that you haven't time to finish the sentence upon which you had embarked.

The symptoms of freezing are that you can't move any part of your body, and don't give a damn.

My experience with Jackson Hole cold got off to an auspicious start in either November or December, the year being 1924 or 1925. (Another symptom of freezing to death is that you can't remember dates; in final stages victims have been known to feel they were fighting the war of 1812.) This was the first time, so far as I know, that I ever had seen, or been in, Jackson Hole, or for that matter in Wyoming, or anywhere near it. I came in over the Teton Pass under the escort of Clay Seaton, about whom I shall have a few words to say later, if I get around to it. We came over this incredible mountain pass in, or rather on, an open sled pulled by six horses and carrying mail, freight, and a Victrola. Clay was driving, and my fellow passengers were Bob Crisp and Ray Ferrin.

The weather on the pass was relatively mild, perhaps a few dozen degrees below zero, but that night it was fifty below in town and the next day it was to drop to sixty-three below by the U.S. Forest Service thermometer, and therefore official, and was to hang between forty-five and fifty for nearly a week.

I checked in at the Crabtree Inn, a small two-story frame structure that was run by Henry and Rose Crabtree, as it still is now in 1955. The rooms were not heated, but the management tried to make up for this by covering the beds with about seven inches of cotton and wool-shoddy blanketing: the news that weight is not necessarily the gauge of insulation value only lately has come over the Continental Divide.

Upon entering my room, which was on the second floor, I estimated in my amateur way that the temperature therein was only about forty below, a clear saving of ten degrees as against the street outside. It was hard getting into bed, working your way into it much as a thin slice of ham must work its way into a drugstore sandwich, a situation aggravated by the fact that once down to your underwear you had only a few seconds in which to save your life.

Presently I was awakened by an over-all ache, generously larded with sudden sharp pains. At first I didn't know what had happened to me—the only certainty was that I wasn't coming down with some rare tropical disease—but when I tried to turn over I got the idea: I was being crushed to death between the mattress and the thick slab of blankets. I arranged myself a little, at the risk of breaking a leg, and got back to sleep, but next I was awakened by an ailment that I at once recognized: my nose was frozen. I withdrew into my sandwich, turtle-like, and it thawed.

Both of these things happened a few more times during the night, then when morning came it brought a worse problem with it. After breaking the ice from around my face, I had to think of getting up. A delicate decision was involved: Should I stay in bed and either starve or just die under pressure or should I get up and try to beat rigor mortis in a photo finish?

I looked around slowly, careful not to break my neck, and saw that my clothes, which I had ripped off in a sort of buzz-saw operation, were all over the room. But at the end of something like an hour, or maybe it was a week, I made up my mind to escape while the escaping was good. In a sudden explosion of my waning strength I rolled the blankets back far enough to allow me to squirm from the vise and stagger to the floor, upon which I was fortunate enough to land upright. After putting my legs through a couple of sleeves and trying to button my pants around my neck I managed somehow to complete this agony; then, flattering myself that I was reasonably presentable, I descended to the lobby with such dignity as I could summon.

This lobby was about twelve feet square. It was dominated, thank God, by a potbellied stove which at the moment was filling the place with stifling, overwhelming, delicious, wonderful heat. The rest of this cubicle was full of people getting dressed. Or, as I at first thought in my confusion, undressed.

Every few minutes another guest would charge in, his arms full of clothes, which he would put on leisurely, taking time out to stretch and yawn, to overheat his behind at the stove, perhaps to present his views on one thing or another: politics, the high cost of living, foreign affairs, the weather . . .

This was the fastest lesson I ever learned, all at one time: you didn't dress in your room.

Now we come to the next subject:

The toilet facilities stood just one hundred and thirty feet from the lobby, due south.

Briefly: Who would be the first to go out and, in a way of speaking, break the ice? *

The attitudes and expressions of those in the lobby ranged from a patently false lightheartedness, intended to remove the individual from competition, to a frank and open grimness, lips set rigidly in manifest determination to wait out the others. A picture of the group could have stood as a composite sketch of Washington preparing to cross the Delaware.

A person I later was to know as Billy Hogan was the first to give up. He rose from a chair in a corner of the lobby. "Well, boys," he said loudly. He laughed a little, not too much. Nor did he engage in any histrionics. With the simplicity commonly found in outstanding figures he buttoned up his sheepskin coat, opened the door without another word or a backward glance, and made his dash.

Everybody moved to, or near, the window that afforded the proper view. Not everybody could see, but it was understood that those in the rear ranks would have the word passed back to them. Fortunately I managed a good position at the window, and saw Mr. Hogan reach his objective safely. In due time he emerged. He began to run, in long strides, not wasting any time that he could help wasting. This was not a wise decision. "Walk!" somebody behind me shouted. At that moment Mr. Hogan stumbled and fell, and, to our horror, came apart at the seams. For one thing, his pants now were wrapped around his ankles.

* In reading this over, I am sorry I said, with respect to breaking the ice, "in a way of speaking." I should have used the word "literally." It is not exactly ice, it is a deep frost that feels like ice. Facing up to this—and now I can say "in a way of speaking"—always has been a problem in Jackson Hole. Many persons have suffered permanent chronic ailments just through waiting for the sun to come up and melt things before venturing out of a morning. This is understandable.

He made no attempt to bring the situation back to normal. He accepted the status quo like a gentleman and jumped, hopped, rolled, scrambled, and otherwise came to port in any manner that seemed a good idea at the moment, this adding up, some old-timers who were present said, to the greatest single performance they ever had witnessed, and they had seen a few cold mornings in their day. Presently Mr. Hogan was among us and we made way and he got to the stove, an imitation Santa Claus but a stout fellow in his own right, breathing deeply . . .

Now the scene went into violent reversal. The idea was to get out there as fast as possible, before the bitter cold reasserted itself with respect to the seat. As I recall it now, Sheriff Jim Francis beat the crowd to the door, followed by Jimmy Fox, a carpenter, who lost . . .

Presently came a huge steaming breakfast at a long table in the dining room. All the guests were men.

Once I remarked, innocently enough, trying to be an amateur native, that it was quite cold out. The table became quiet. My colleagues looked at me, then at a person I later was to know as a scientist in the employ of the U.S. Fish and Wildlife Service. He cleared his throat. "This is a very dry cold," he said. "I venture to say that it's no colder out right now, in point of actual discomfort, than it would be in a place like let's say Chicago at ten or fifteen above. It's all a matter of moisture in the air. You can hardly feel the cold here."

"I felt at least some of it last night," I suggested.

"You only thought so," several people said.

All right, I only thought so. I felt bitter, and reserved comment. But upon thinking it over I said, "Look, the way I learned it in school, when the cold takes hold of a person all that counts is the thermometer. When it comes to freezing the liquids that make up much of the human body, it's strictly a matter of temperature. Is it your point that should a man accidentally freeze to death here he wouldn't be considered dead because the cold is so dry?"

Somebody said, "Oh no, the guy would be dead all right. I mean, he wouldn't just thaw out in the spring and go on about his business just like nothing had happened."

Rose Crabtree was standing there listening, her backside to the stove, taking up much room. She said, "Oh, cut it out. Now I'll tell you, a fellow came in here last winter, he was a salesman. I can't remember what for, something that would save you money if you bought it, and he got a room but he was a sissy and about daybreak he got up and came down to the lobby to get warm. Old Man Leek had come in a few minutes before from the South Park country on snowshoes in a blizzard and he was all covered with ice and frost and snow and was standing by the stove. The salesman looked at him and said, 'Good morning, partner. What room did you have last night?' "

Nobody laughed. Rose had addressed this mostly to me, and I said, "Mrs. Crabtree, if you please. I heard that twenty years ago. It's supposed to have happened everyplace in the West."

She shrugged. "Okay. Nevertheless this is the one place it actually happened. Now I'll tell you one I'm sure you never heard. Every morning at breakfast, here, in the winter, and not all of you boys know this," she said, looking around, "I check the register against the orders of ham and eggs to see if anybody is missing. We've never found anybody in one of our beds in April, left over from December, but I'm taking no chances."

It was agreed that Rose had won the discussion.

Breakfast broke up and a couple of Forest Service men went to their office and one or two others left but most of us moved into the lobby for the day. In a few minutes one of the

Forest Service men phoned and said it was sixty-three below zero.

Later some cowboys came into town with a bunch of about two hundred Hereford steers, driving them someplace or other. They parked the steers in the town square and put up their horses and came into the lobby. They were so stiff they hardly could walk, and thawed out at the stove. I never had seen people so cold, alive.

"How is she out?" somebody asked.

The cowboys looked at him, whoever it was, I have forgotten. "It is chilly," one of them said.

Rose was there. "Why are you driving in this weather?" she asked.

"No brains," one of the cowboys said. "No sense at all."

They went on into the dining room.

We stood at the window looking at the steers. They were standing perfectly still and close together, as animals do in extreme cold in order not to disturb the thin blanket of warm air held in suspense in the hairs of their hides.

"Sixty-three is colder than I've seen it here in town since I don't know when," Sheriff Jim Francis said. He yawned. "Well, one thing's a cinch. If any crime is committed around here today, anything I have to handle, they'll have to come over here to do it . . ."

I was in Jackson to write a story about the elk herd. I phoned the headquarters of the Government Elk Refuge and talked with Almer Nelson, the superintendent, whom I never had met. We agreed to wait until the weather warmed a bit before getting together, especially since I had some work to do in town anyway, so I stayed at the Crabtree two more days, then the thermometer got around to the subtropical reading of only forty-five below and Almer drove in with a team and a bobsled to pick me up for a week's stay at the refuge.

After he had introduced himself and had soaked up a little warmth we went out and got into the rig. He looked at me and said, "You better take off your mittens." I didn't know what he meant; I figured my hands weren't going to be any too warm the way they were. He noticed my confusion. "This is a dry cold," he said, clucking to the horses, "and you think you're getting along fine but then you find your face frozen, behind your back."

"What?" I said.

"I mean," he said, "it sneaks up on you when you don't expect it. Everything is wonderful, then you try to smile and can't, you have no cheeks. You start to say something and your lips don't move. So you take your mittens off and put your hands under your armpits and keep bringing them out, alternately, and touch them quickly to various parts of your face."

He showed me how, and we rode the two long slow miles to the refuge through drifted snow that held the horses to a walk, moving our hands, as though in a trance, from armpits to nose and return for more warmth—the cheeks and eyelids and lips, and back again, in a continuous rhythmic movement as though we were taking part in some weird African tribal dance, perhaps, in slow motion.*

We got to the Government ranch without any mishap other

* I hesitate in writing this footnote for fear some of the readers of this book, if there are any readers, will feel I am being indelicate. I certainly am not. I am trying to project the realities of winter life in Jackson Hole. Well, the two warmest parts of the human body, the last to freeze, are the armpits and the crotch. This latter is the warmer of the two. It is ordinary practice, in the very coldest weather, to thrust one's hands through the pants pockets and warm them in the crotch, bringing this momentary heat out to the face, just as I have described. Every spring Mr. C. C. Cummins, the town tailor and for many years, as at present, also the town clerk, has to repair scores of pairs of pants with the pockets broken out. His job is not as easy as you think. The silver dollar is the basic medium of exchange in the West. The pockets must be made of fabric that is tough enough to withstand the wear and tear of these silver dollars in summer, yet fragile enough to be pushed through by the human hand when a person finds himself in peril, come winter. Thank you.

than a slight indiscretion at the tip of my nose, an organ which never was fashioned, either in size or in shape, for a Wyoming winter. I was mighty glad to get there. I looked forward to my visit, not only because I had taken an instant liking to Almer (this has lasted thirty-one years, as of this writing) and wanted to see the elk but because I figured there would be a vast difference between the Government quarters and the Crabtree Inn, on the side of creature comfort. For once I was in favor of bureaucracy extending its ugly tentacles into every crevice and corner of the United States, especially Jackson Hole, wasting the taxpayers' money right and left on modern conveniences, with emphasis on heating plants.

Mrs. Nelson unfortunately was out for the evening, visiting nearby relatives, but Almer came up with a swell supper of steak and baked potatoes, and afterward we enjoyed a few bottles of beer, courtesy of President Coolidge, as we sat before a hot stove and relaxed. Almer said his wife would be home late, and he was going to wait up, but I became very drowsy and asked to retire. My room was just off the living room and the door was open, to let the heat in. As I entered, however, I was conscious of a certain deadly chill, an ominous note, and when I saw the vast bulk of the blankets on the bed I knew I was up against it still once more, and President Coolidge could take his beer and he knew what he could do with it.

When I woke up in the morning, having again thawed my nose a few times during the night by holding it under the covers, I at least now had the advantage of knowing the ropes, the Jackson Hole way of life as exemplified at the Crabtree. I slipped out of bed sideways, grabbed my clothes and dashed out into the other room, where the stove was. Upon doing this I found myself, clad in an oversized and by no means clean suit of wool underwear, drooping badly in various places, facing a beautiful and fully dressed lady.

I flatter myself that I was equal to the occasion.

I bowed a little, dropping a shoe. "Mrs. Nelson?" I inquired.

"Yes," she said. "Good morning, Mr. Hough, it's so nice to see you. I'm sorry I missed you last night, but I came in rather late. How did you sleep?"

"Wonderfully, thanks," I said. "You have a nice place, here." I glanced out the window, or rather the small portion of it that wasn't covered with frost. "Look at the sunlight on those hills. A magnificent country."

"We think so," she said.

I decided to dress, but in trying to get my pants on one-handed I dropped my other shoe and the pants fell to my ankles.

"God damn it to hell!" I said inadvertently. "Excuse me, Mrs. Nelson."

"Perfectly all right," she assured me. "Now just make yourself at home, and I'll start breakfast. Do you like waffles?"

"My favorite," I said. She left for the kitchen and I dressed for breakfast, the first time I ever heard of anybody doing that.

I soon discovered the basic difference between the living room of the Government ranch and the lobby of the Crabtree, with respect to heat, which at the moment was very near to being an obsession with me.*

The private-enterprise stove in the Crabtree was large enough to hold a fire overnight, if properly fed and banked. The statist, or paternalistic, little bit of scrap iron in the Government house, probably known as 10442A, Stove, Iron,

* Sometimes when I tell people about Jackson Hole I get an uneasy feeling that they feel I am being coy about, or in any case greatly exaggerating, the chill winter weather. I therefore hereby quote verbatim from the February 1, 1951, issue of the Jackson's Hole *Courier:*

Other things besides prices and wages were frozen around these parts this week. Sunday night a cold wave came down from the north and everything, including people, almost congealed.

The coldest official reading in this locality was at Bondurant this morning, when the government thermometer read –57. Tuesday it had showed a –56 Mrs. Walt Floerke reported, and added that it was slow to rise, staying in the minus 40's most of the forenoon.

Official forest office recordings were a minus 28 Sunday night and minus

Cast, evidently was designed by the Department of Agriculture, which did not want its confounded forests burned up any faster than necessary. It would hold any given fire about two hours and ten minutes. As a consequence of this, the fire had to be started, from scratch, every morning.

Almer and I took turns. At first, never knowing where or when my hostess was going to pop up, ready for the opera, I dressed in my room, then went out and made the fire. I later learned that the proper procedure was to disentangle yourself from the bed, dash out and start the fire, then dive back into bed and await developments, usually waffles.

One morning I asked Almer, "Why do you have such a small stove, that won't hold a fire overnight?"

"I have a larger one coming," he said. "I have filled out a form, a requisition, explaining the circumstances. It ought to be along any day now. I think the requisition is being processed in Washington."

"How long ago did you send it in?" I asked.

"About three years," Almer said . . .

I shall never forget the next six days. Most of the elk were down, some 12,000 of them, but even now others were drifting in from the hills. I watched the feeding of the elk, from hayracks; Almer and I stood on the top of a nearby small butte and watched the elk below us slowly milling over the refuge area, and beyond, like live cinnamon on the white frosting

---

34 Monday night. Tuesday night it was –27, and this morning at 7:00 it was –32, the lowest point reached during the 24 hour period.

The Reclamation Service official readings at Moran the past four mornings are:

Monday morning, –46; Tuesday, –48; Wednesday, –36; and today, –50. Elt Davis' thermometer at Jackson Lake ranger station showed a minus 52 Tuesday morning, but we have not heard from him today. The official temperature at Grand Teton National Park Tuesday a.m. was 41½, but Elt reported from there in the afternoon that a heat wave had struck and the reading was then only 16 below.

West Yellowstone was reported to be virtually stymied after Sunday night's minus reading in the 50's, with oil and prestone frozen in the inhabitants' cars.

of a cake. Almer explained that they hadn't settled down yet, but would do so later, scarcely moving as they awaited the relief of spring. Again one evening, during a light snowstorm, in the moonlight, I saw several hundred come down out of the hills, and into the refuge, a memorable sight . . .

One day Almer said, "Well, I suppose you're anxious to get out into the field."

This confused me. "What have we been doing this past week?" I asked. "Haven't we been out in the field?"

This seemed to amuse Almer. "This is a large country," he said (unconsciously quoting President Coolidge, our bartender). "There are pockets of wintering elk all through the mountains. The largest one is up on the Gros Ventre River, where the canyon broadens out above Slide Lake. You'll want to see that. It isn't far, about thirty-two miles from here. I saw Jimmy Simpson in the post office the other day and he's going up there any day now, to the Redmond ranch on Crystal Creek, and he said he'd be glad to have you go along, if you want to. He's a big-game guide, the best around."

"Well, I don't know," I said. "These elk have seen a lot of me lately. I'd hate to wear out my welcome."

"The ones up there are different," Almer said. "They won't even know who you are." He looked out the window. "Only thirty-five below zero this morning," he said happily. "Smells like spring. I'll bet we have a short winter."

chapter 16

A Delightful Excursion

WHY DID Jimmy Simpson want to go up to the Redmond ranch on Crystal Creek? It is quite true that Mrs. Redmond was his sister, that she was in California, and that he had promised to drop in at the ranch now and then to see that everything was in order. Is traveling thirty-two miles in way-below-zero weather "dropping in," and anyway what could go wrong at the ranch, which had no livestock, the whole thing frozen stiff as a board in any case? Perhaps he just wanted to see if the confounded place still was there, as though anybody would want to steal it at this time of year. In a word, why couldn't Jimmy Simpson mind his own business and let me alone?

"It's getting warmer out," Jimmy said, "and I figure on starting out early in the morning. Want to come along?"

I looked at the stove, which was glowing a dull red. In a country where men are so confoundedly men, I was trapped. "Why," I said heartily, "of course I want to go! It's wonderful of you to ask me! Be sure," I added lightly, "that you have plenty of antifreeze in the radiator. It's only a couple of hundred below zero now, but we may run into a cold spell."

Jimmy looked at me curiously.

"What radiator?" he asked.

I could feel my stomach melting within me, for now I knew the worst . . .

Once more I was up against my old enemy, the common horse.

It is a fact of history, just as the date of the Battle of Tours is, that the first horses the American Indian ever saw were those ridden by De Soto, coming up from the mouth of the Mississippi River, and by Coronado and his small army, moving in from Mexico. Many ignorant people, which certainly does not include me, think that the Plains Indians invented the horse, but if you want the facts the encyclopedia is at your disposal. The Indians, as soon as they had stolen enough horses to make it pay, merely became the best riders the world ever has known.

The riding habit worn by these early Frenchmen and Spaniards was an elaborate affair, featuring a kind of leather skirt, and the saddles had many fancy trappings, the net result being that the horse and the rider blended into what appeared to be a single animal, and that is what the Indians thought it was. When for the first time they saw a rider dismount, they fainted, or whatever the Indian equivalent is, because they thought the animal had broken in two, and both parts were alive.*

Riding instructors, both amateur and professional, used to tell me, and other pupils of course, "You must get the feeling that you are a part of your horse."

They do not say *what* part of the horse, and anyway I say the hell with it. My idea is not to become a part of any horse, but to get as far away from it as I can, without appearing rude.

Every time I see one, which is no oftener than I can help, I experience a sense of shock, or at least of surprise, at the sheer fact of its being among us. What is it doing here? Why didn't it go down the drain with the Flood, as many important mammalogists think it should have, and leave us alone?

* I am sorry I cannot give my source here. I came across this several times while doing research work on the Chisholm Trail at the University of Texas, at Austin, and the University of Oklahoma, at Norman, in 1947.

This dumb heathen relic has no business here at all. As a matter of fact the twin terms "dumb brutes" and "dumb animals" probably stem from the horse, the original of which, it lately has been established, was just eighteen inches high. It should have stayed there, although it couldn't even bark, and still can't.

I have ridden a good many horses—full-size ones, or more than full size—in a considerable number of places, but I never have done it on purpose, just for the ride. When I joined the Army in 1917 I had no way of knowing that we still were fighting Geronimo, involving horses, and I still don't know whether I was under orders to ride a horse, or the horse was under orders to throw me off. It worked out about fifty-fifty. The horse never helped me get on, but he always helped me get off: I spent just as much time looking at horse's bellies as I did looking at their backs, and before I was through I began to get horses and hospitals all mixed up. Asked to describe a horse at that time, I might well have said that the horse was white-enameled, had a sheet on it, could be cranked up to a sitting position, and was attended by an Army nurse.

"We'll have a fine warm place up there," Jimmy said, "as soon as we get a fire going. It will be our base of operations. Let's see, thirty-two miles, we can make it in a day; I've done it many times before."

"Probably alone," I suggested. "This time you have a guest. My standard time for thirty-two miles, on a horse, is one week."

"I've got a good horse for you," said Almer Nelson, who was present at this meeting, which more and more I began to look at as a funeral service, "and you won't have any trouble."

"What time do we start?" I asked Jimmy.

"About dawn," he said.

I took this news in stride. As it happened, this would have

been my morning to start the fire, and by leaving at dawn I was well out of it. So we parted, and I went to bed. Getting up at dawn was a cinch, because I had been awake a long time before that, phrasing, in my mind, various paragraphs of my will. I also was thinking things over. What did Jimmy mean by "base of operations"? Were we going to climb Mount Everest, or what? Did he mean that as soon as we should get the fire started at Crystal Creek, and thaw out, we would have to go outdoors again? The stay there was to be about four days, he had said. Would I have to go out looking for elk every day or would I get a day off, to freeze to death in comfort in the God damn ranch house? *

Up at dawn, a fine breakfast of several cups of hot coffee and a waffle, then Jimmy came along, and we got ready for the ride. I was introduced to my horse, and we were off. The first fifty yards were not bad at all, in fact rather pleasant, but then my legs began to freeze and along with this freezing came an extremely painful condition around the knees, due perhaps to the unusual shape of the horse, which was round, or, to be accurate about it, cylindrical.

I was hoping that my legs would freeze solid, in shape, thus reducing the excruciating pain in my knees, but this never quite happened, so from time to time I dismounted and walked, although I realized I was in constant danger of having my legs break off at the knee, the hips, or—as it sometimes seemed to me—at the neck. After each walk my legs would get almost straight again, so I could get back onto the horse and let them refreeze—still not quite

* At this point I shall have to ask the reader to give me the benefit of the doubt, whatever that means. Up until ten days before this I never had seen an elk, outside of a saloon, never had seen a mountain, my familiarity with the West was limited to looking at wooden Indians in front of cigar stores. Later, over a period of some thirty years in and out of Jackson Hole, the situation changed somewhat. In writing about these earlier experiences, I hope you will not think I am trying to be funny. Once in St. Paul, Minnesota, I spent a night and a day in jail. My friends thought that my unfortunate incarceration was a huge joke, but I was the one who was in jail, just as in this case I was the one, not you, who had to ride the horse to Crystal Creek.

solid enough so that I could forget them—in semicircles.

Sometime during the day we came to the ranch of Guil Huff, Doc Huff's brother, and went in. I was very happy about this. Upon being introduced to the Huffs I attempted a slight bow, which of course was a mistake. We had lots of hot coffee and half a bale of hay for lunch, and I rested on a couch, wishing with all my heart and soul that I could stay there forever and ever and ever.

I slept for about ten seconds, then here was Jimmy again, and after thanking the Huffs for their hospitality—for the only time in my life I wished I were a millionaire, so I could buy the ranch—I had to be my real self again. Richard the Lion Hearted, and get on that son of a bitch of a horse.

We went on and on. My knees now were hurting me as I never had hurted before, excepting only once, when I was six years old and got caught stealing a piece of chocolate cake from the pantry. I kept getting off the horse and back on again in a sort of vague equestrian photomontage; I couldn't keep track of where I was, and after a month or so we came to Crystal Creek, and the ranch house, and Jimmy made the fire and I slept on the floor, afraid to sleep in a bed, which would cause me to bend in the middle and probably break into a million pieces.

In the morning, whenever that was, I was invited to take a ride out and look over the elk situation. Fortunately I had a pair of binoculars with me, and I crawled out to a nearby ridge and looked over the elk, and later, as an outstanding expert, wrote one of the most learned and comprehensive articles on the Gros Ventre section of the Jackson Hole elk herd ever to appear in print.

But the hell with this.

Let's change the subject.

Next chapter, please . . .

chapter 17

The Big Hill

AS WINTER progresses, Teton Pass, figuratively speaking, grows higher, and higher, and higher, and certainly more important. You can almost forget it is there in summer, but now the focus is sharp and thin.

Locally referred to as The Hill, for decades it was the Hole's only connection with the outside world, and this was a tenuous one, indeed, not only because of the difficulties inherent in crossing that formidable range of mountains but also because once you had managed to get over into Idaho all you had was the dinky one-train-a-day railhead at Victor, subject to declassification in winter to a one-a-week or even a one-a-month train.

The age of the highway truck has changed this last factor, the road has been vastly improved, but nobody has done anything about the weather, and The Hill itself is as sinister as ever, never out of the minds and calculations of the people of Jackson Hole in its dual role as both a threat and a blessing, in being.

From the Hole side the road winds upward at various angles, often distressingly approaching the vertical, the switchbacks stacked up five and six deep below you as you squirm toward the summit. The top of the pass is a flat place just large enough for a control cabin, a barn, and a yard for teams to turn around in. From this platform the road drops into Idaho as precipitously as it came up out of Wyoming, then presently levels off a bit and the last several miles are easy on the nerves.

When Jackson Hole first was settled the Pass road was no more than a trail: there were places where wagons had to be dismantled and the parts lashed to the backs of the horses. In early days, mail and supplies often were carried over the Tetons by men on snowshoes, and even today brigades of men with shovels, snowplows or no snowplows, occasionally have to leave their homes or their ranches to pitch in to keep The Hill open, although in spite of all efforts it frequently is closed.

One time Dick Winger and George Kelly decided to introduce pigs to the Hole and sent to Iowa for five of them as a starter. They picked them up at Victor and loaded them into their sled and started over the mountains. Everything went smoothly enough until they came to the final struggle just below the crest of the Pass.

The horses now were taking the steep grade in short hitches. George was driving and Dick was behind, scoring the sled: he stuck a shovel into the snow and ice at the end of a rear runner to keep the sled in place whenever the horses stopped to rest. But just as they were closing in on their goal the horses fell down and the whole rig, horses and all, started back down the hill. Gaining speed, it came up against a tree. The impact popped the endgate open and spilled the pigs.

The only thing that had to be done now was to put the pigs back into the sled-box, rechain the endgate, and continue. Dick picked up one of the pigs, all of whom, or which, seemed surprised at what had happened, and hoisted it. (I forgot to say, these were little pigs. I don't know what a little pig is called, but these were the same as a calf would be to a cow, or a colt to a horse, a cub to a bear, and so on.) But a pig is slippery-shaped, even when it's dry, kind of like a balloon is, and Dick lost his hold on it and it got away.

This stirred up whatever small intellect a pig has, and it began to run, in the only possible direction at the moment: downhill. The other pigs followed.

Dick went after them as fast as he could, but when it comes to running downhill there is no substitute for a pig, for a pig can roll even faster than it can run, and after Dick had fallen down a few times, losing ground, he decided he was at a disadvantage. In a word, he was playing the other fellow's game. It was time to use his head, if he could.

At this point there were several switchbacks in the road, and Dick got the idea of short-cutting the pigs by plunging through the snow to a lower level, where he could meet them head on. At first the pigs, using diversionary tactics, got past him, but at the next switchback he caught one. He was quite pleased, but the flush of victory paled when he realized that he was stuck with the pig. He stood there thinking it over (meanwhile of course the other pigs were on their way) and finally an idea hit him. He knew nothing about pigs, but he felt, by instinct, that if you throw a pig into a snowbank it might not know what to do. He tried it, and it worked. The pig kicked its pretty little feet a few times, wriggled its little behind, grunted, and went to sleep. Dick now knew more about pigs than he had known before.

By cutting across lots, so to speak, always meeting the pigs coming toward him, and concentrating with all his might and main on one pig at a time—his first error had been in trying to concentrate on all of them—he finally had all five pigs in snowdrifts. The job now was to get them to the top of the Pass. George Kelly, backtracking on foot after he had secured the horses, joined him. They accomplished their task in a matter of a few hours simply by leapfrogging one pig over the other. That is to say, they lifted the lowest pig out of the snow, carried it beyond the next pig, and threw it back into the snow, then kept repeating this exhausting labor until they had all the pigs back to the sled.

Just in the interest of telling a story (without wishing for any further hard luck to Dick and George), I should like to be able to say that at the last minute one of the pigs got loose and ran all the way back to the railroad. But since I am confined in this book to the truth I cannot indulge myself in this delightful fantasy.

In any case the terrific work these heroes put in on the Pass largely was wasted. Long before they got all the pigs back to the sled they pantingly had agreed to get the hell out of the pig business as fast as they could, upon reaching Jackson Hole. They carried out this program with precision and dispatch.*

It is no coincidence that St. John's Hospital, in Jackson, its second-largest structure, a beautiful log building set in its own park, is one of the finest and best-staffed in Wyoming, attracting clients from the cities of eastern Idaho and even from Salt Lake City, in Utah. It has been endowed with plenty of dough, over the years, thanks to the generosity of wealthy dudes and some of the ranchers and merchants. But its proximity to Teton Pass, many think, has done more than anything else to put it on easy street.

Its exterior beauty is matched by an immaculate and well-equipped interior, which is a good idea, because many of the patients, especially if they had tried to come in over Teton Pass, see the inside of it quite a while before they see the outside. Here is the law of supply and demand in full flower,

* As of the fall of 1955, Dick Winger is secretary of the Jackson Hole Chamber of Commerce. Occasionally he gets a letter inquiring about the situation in the Hole with respect to raising pigs. Dick handles this delicately. In his official capacity he says that this is an ideal pig place. Then as a man of conscience and of honor, he always adds, in paraphrase of the classic recipe for making a rabbit stew, "First, of course, you must catch your pig . . ."

a virtually perfect example of natural regional adjustment.

The advent of the rotary plow has removed many of the hazards of the crossing in winter, by professionals, but in the summer the tourists, in common with all advocates of the horseless buggy, look at a better road as an invitation to disaster.

The hospital is building a new wing.

The over-all story of the Pass is that of men and horses. I don't know, and never did know, any of the horses, but in my mind the greatest driver of them all was Clay Seaton, who brought me in on the mail stage so I could spend a few memorable nights at the Crabtree and a few more at the Government ranch, then make my historic ride to Crystal Creek with Jimmy Simpson.

Clay also took me out, some weeks later in the winter.

We were to leave the post office early in the morning and I got there well ahead of time, for the trick was to glom onto a sack of first-class mail for your seat, and let latecomers try to hatch out the sharp-edged parcel post and even sharper-edged express and freight. There were four passengers, besides me: a cowboy, a preacher, and a lady with a small child. The preacher had a saddle horse, complete with English saddle, that he was taking outside to winter while he vacationed in the Southwest. He tied the horse on behind the stage.

We got away to a fine start, everybody full of hot coffee and, with the exception of the preacher and the child, an off-the-record slug of gin; clear cold weather, and so on. But as we mounted the Pass over the sharp switchbacks, skirting the canyon, we ran into the very hell of a blizzard, just about blowing us off the stage.*

* In the Hole itself, it was—and still is—customary to travel in covered rigs in winter. Upon the sled is superimposed a canvas hood, looking just like the covered wagons you see in the movies. Often there is a stove in this, the smokestack going up through the canvas. But during the days when the

Then the lead team went off the road.

You take a ledge or notch road, cut into the side of a hill, the snow always packs up against the cut bank and edges out over the canyon side of the road. This outer snow of course has no ground beneath it, and if you walk on it, especially if you are a horse, you are likely to get a surprise. Clay had been watching for this, but the blizzard really was crowding in, and when we were a scant four hundred yards from the top, starting an especially steep pull, the off-horse went down, then pulled his mate along, and they were out of luck. They were held in suspension partly by the snow and partly by the pole team, but the die was cast and Clay had to cut the traces with his clasp knife, and the two horses rolled down the side of the canyon, out of sight in the storm. We went down and found them, in very deep snow. Only the nose of the under horse was showing. Clay, who knew the canyon and the snow by heart, figured that if we could release them from the snow they could get back, going slantwise clear to the top of the Pass. We returned to the stage, which, as all stages were and still are—even the trucks—was equipped with axes, shovels, and blankets.

All of us except the lady and the preacher took shovels and went down to the horses. The preacher came along to watch. With our shovels we first dug around the head of the under horse, and went on from there. As we were working we became aware of a sound other than that of the wind through the pine trees and the noise of the blizzard generally.

It was the preacher, standing there intoning directions, in detail. We kept digging and he kept talking. In time we came to the point at which the horses would have to show some cooperation if they were to get out. It is unusual for

Teton Pass mail stage was horse-drawn—it now of course is motorized—you couldn't have these comforts. Should the rig be hit by a snowslide, or just go off the road and turn over a few times, everybody would be trapped, at best, and, at worst, cooked. You had to have jumping space.

a horse to do this. Any horse, caught in deep snow—and the snow may be no deeper than up to his belly—will stand still and wait for his body to be found in the spring, or his skeleton to be found years later. He will mire down, permanently, in mud up to his knees. The trick in digging a horse out is to keep him standing until he is cleared, for a horse always confuses lying down with death itself; even on a city street a horse needs the help of everything this side of a bulldozer to get up. Wonderful animal.

Of course, it must be admitted that the horse has something on his side. What is he going to get up for? What is he going back to? What the hell fun does a horse have? A horse is always pulling something in which he has no immediate interest, or somebody is always sitting on his back, to escape having to walk by himself. Having his body found next spring probably seems as reasonable to a horse as having it found any other spring.

Although the horse, in the broader view, doesn't give a damn, it will respond, doubtless in sheer appeasement, just hoping the noise will stop and night will come, to human persuasion.

This persuasion includes the vocal. No wonder Clay Seaton always has been one of the great teamsters of modern times. If there was, or is, a better talker-to-horses than Clay, he hasn't shown up yet. In volume alone, Clay is a kind of animated Public Address System, although he relies mostly on quality. I bitterly regret that publishing practice prevents me from pointing up Clay's position. He often uses the rare and difficult intersyllable system. One of the first times I ever was fired by a newspaper city editor he said it was because I was "too goddam inde goddam pendent." This is fourth-rate Seaton, of course. The things Clay can say to a horse shouldn't be said to a dog. I am not sure that any man ever became famous because of his ability to swear but on the other hand I never have known one to become famous for his ability *not* to swear, so it comes out a tie. In any case, it is my belief that every man, in his chosen calling, reaches one peak moment in his career, a summit never again quite to be attained. I believe I can say, in all humility, that I was with Clay Seaton when, on Teton Pass in that January of 1925, he stood upon the thin sharp edge of immortality.*

Well, back to the job.

We had come to the point, in digging the snow away from the horses, at which with our further help they could be saved, or rather save themselves, to return still once more to a life of debasement and drudgery.

The climactic moment, that is to say, was at hand.

Clay now turned to the preacher, whose impatience with our efforts, coupled with instructions of his own, had increasingly become more voluble. Using the most refined English he knew, Clay suggested that the preacher get the hell back to the stage, sit down, and keep his trap shut. "I have all respect for the cloth," Clay said in effect, "but I ask you to leave us alone. I now shall have to mention a few things to these horses, in my own vernacular, with which

* The only person Clay Seaton ever acknowledged as matching him was Countess Gyzika. She was the only one he ever turned the reins over to on the Pass, and the only one he ever let talk to his horses. "I owe her much," Clay still admits. "She didn't teach me all I knew in talking to horses, but she sure as hell gave me a few wonderful new ideas." The Countess, née Eleanor (Cissy) Patterson, of the publishing dynasty (Washington *Times-Herald,* Chicago *Tribune,* New York *Daily News*), daughter of Medill Patterson, had married Count Gyziki in Chicago when she was twenty, then lived in Poland, where her daughter, Felicia, now of Washington, was born. She later divorced Count Gyziki, and first came to Jackson Hole in 1920, in her private railroad car, which she left at Victor, Idaho, in search of complete peace and quiet so she could orient herself to a new concept of life. She built a beautiful place near the head of Flat Creek. She told her friend, Evie Robert, "I have seen taller mountains and larger lakes, but the people here I love." This affection was returned by Jackson Hole. She could give and take. She made the grade with everybody. According to Rose Crabtree, her intimate friend for many years, when Cissy Patterson was dying in 1948 she ordered her private car for a terminal trip to Jackson Hole, and the car was made ready in the Washington railroad yards, but by then it was too late.

you may not agree, and which may be shocking to your ears."

The preacher looked at Clay and Clay looked at the preacher and the preacher got going.

Clay now took a deep breath, and starting talking to the horses . . .

When the horses were back on the road, Clay took them up to the control station at the top of the Pass, and brought back replacements. We had been delayed only about two hours, and there still was a chance to make it to the railroad by midnight. So we kept going, and stopped at Bircher's ranch, on the Idaho side, for a short period of rest and refreshment.

During this pull the preacher sat alone at the tailgate of the sled, staring moodily at his horse and thinking God-knew-what. Perhaps the wind had brought to him the exact words of Clay's imprecations to the horses; in any case, he seemed glum. When we got to Bircher's the rest of us sat at the family board, but the preacher sat apart, saying his own grace in lonely splendor.

In spite of its drawbacks and its discomforts and its dangers—and aside from its own peculiar dramatic charm—Teton Pass has laid the foundation for several modest fortunes in Jackson. The rate for hauling freight in from Victor, Idaho, always has been a penny a pound. Supposing this to consist of goods shipped in to the merchants, for sale, the cost of the freight always has been added to the retail price. Or, to put it in its true light, more accurately, the retail cost has been added to the freight charge. What I am trying to say is that the freight cost of one penny a pound often was in itself marked up to show a profit of up to 2,000 per cent before the cost or the selling price of the merchandise itself even was considered.

In a word, the residents of Jackson Hole have bought

Teton Pass, lock, stock, and barrel, about a hundred times, and it should have been deeded to them years ago. When it comes to multiple sales, the Brooklyn Bridge isn't even in the running.

When Berry and I first were in Jackson we traded with Joe Jones, one of the two grocers in town. Joe had a small place on the square, although it wasn't much of a square then, and he handled odds and ends of things besides just groceries. Joe operated under just one business slogan, which he never tired of intoning, especially when making out his bills. "It's all got to be brought over The Hill," he'd say, quietly and firmly tripling the price. I remember one item Berry always bought, cornflakes. The price then was ten cents a package. Joe's price was a quarter.

If you asked him to estimate the cost of bringing in a package of cornflakes, weight eight ounces, at the rate of a penny a pound, he would get lost in a mathematical maze, figuring in the weight of the cardboard carton, the weight of the wooden crates, a certain amount of wet snow that may have clung to the crate, and so on, finally giving up but still declaring he was losing on the deal: you could take the cornflakes or leave them.

Joe Jones hated the grocery business with every fiber of his being. He was a writer by preference and, to a very real extent, in fact. In a corner of the incredibly overcrowded back room, or shed, attached to the store proper, he had a small stove, a table, a chair, and a typewriter. There he did the thing he wanted to do, and never mind the store. When he was at work in his study and a customer entered the store, supposing one or the other of his daughters not to be on duty, he was furious, cutting old friends to the quick as he scarcely spoke, angrily adding still another nickel to the cornflakes, hoping to heaven they'd take their lousy trade to the other store.

I met Joe after I had been in Jackson only a few days, back in 1925, when I was there to write that series of pieces on the elk herd, and while chatting with Joe he mentioned that he did a little writing himself. Without too much urging he opened the safe and brought out a roll of magazines and took the rubber bands from them and showed them to me.

These were copies of the *Saturday Evening Post* and they contained a series called "Following the Gold Camps." I had read and thoroughly enjoyed these pieces when they appeared; they were outstanding in my memory, and I recalled wondering, when I read them, if I ever could hope to write something for the *Post*. Joe had been a professional gambler for years, a poker player, and he had traveled the West doing just what the title of his *Post* pieces said. He also had written a series for the same magazine called "My Bet with Uncle Sam," which recounted his experiences in taking up his homestead in Jackson Hole.

At present he was writing for *Western Magazine* and one or two others. And he certainly could write. I don't think I've ever read better descriptive English when he was on his favorite subject, the beauty and drama of the country in which he lived.

One day in his shed he was reading to me from something he had written—and he could read as beautifully as he could write. A couple of customers came into the store, up front. Joe stopped reading, leaned back a little so they couldn't see him through the partly open door, and placed a finger at his lips.

"Be quiet," he whispered to me. "They'll soon go away."

chapter 18

My House Is on Fire

WILLIE KUHRTZ, although he meant well, was slow in bringing me the various things I needed for my cabin, and he never did come through with the Chinese chopsticks, the cannon for the front yard, or the Oriental rugs. He fell flat on his face with respect to the elk steaks (2 inches) but that was because he was out of elk. Mayor Harry Clissold, however, came to my rescue in this last particular. Harry owns, and with his wife, Berta, operates, the Jackson Cold Storage Company, which handles a lot of wild game, as many as eight hundred elk in a season, processing and quick-freezing them, and any time he can't come up with a stray elk steak it's funny.*

One bleak day in late January, Harry presented me with a wonderful elk steak ($1^{15}/_{16}$ inches thick) and I decided to prepare an elaborate supper for myself, with this as the piece of resistance, as it is called in Paris, and opened a can of corn, heated up some leftover wild rice, and polished up two red apples, for looks and general nostalgia.

I used both plates of my electric contrivance, also turned

* Since I left Jackson last, Harry and Roy Jensen twice have sent me considerable amounts of wild meat, packed in dry ice. I have had to put this in the cold room at my butcher's, since I do not have a deep freeze. The last time, the butcher called me and said, "Your wild meat is bleeding, through the carton." I thought it over. "Get some Band-Aid," I suggested. "But the blood is green," the butcher said. I went over there and we opened the carton. Harry and Roy thoughtfully had included a bottle of Crème de Menthe, and it had somehow got broken.

on all the lights in the room, for a festive air. I took the things off the little stove when they were done and placed them on my table. At this very instant the lights went out. This did not disturb me too much. The lights periodically went out all over Jackson for technical reasons, and lights failed in individual establishments for reasons both technical and financial. I got out a couple of candles and lit them and began my meal.

I now smelled something new in the room: in a word, smoke. Glancing around, I noticed that this came from behind the wallboard with which the cabin was lined.

Fortunately I had a fire extinguisher, small size, holding about a quart of gasoline, or whatever fire extinguishers have in them. This was part of Willie's equipment—one that he was proud of, always mentioning the fact of its presence when I complained about other things. I took the extinguisher from its rack, placed it on my table, sat down and lit a cigarette. I knew I had a fire on my hands, all right, but I didn't know where it was. At one time I caught a flicker of flame, in addition to the smoke, but it was like heat lightning: indefinite, impossible to pin down. By the light of my candles I killed time by reading the directions on the fire extinguisher.

Presently, to my relief, the wallboard began to turn black at a spot just over my bed, and since this spot was on a direct line between an electric outlet and a place where the wires came out of the wallboard, I felt quite sure that the fire was due to faulty wiring. I now had something to get my teeth into and I got up on my bed, with the fire extinguisher, and with the butt end of it—having no ax—knocked out the charred part of the wallboard. Now I could see the fire, which was in the logs. I put out the fire and resumed my dinner, which was getting cold. I had taken scarcely a mouthful when I happened to notice that the fire was back again. I returned to my bed and looked it over, through the smoke. A fire in logs, especially if the logs are as old as these were, is hard to handle. Big old logs crack as they dry over the years, and some of these cracks may be as wide as an inch at the circumference of the log. So the fire not only can work its way between the logs, but into the logs themselves.

I filled a large saucepan with water and threw it at the fire. After repeating this a few times, the fire seemed to be out once more, and my bed was wet. Going after the water reminded me that there was a bottle of whiskey on the window sill of the bathroom, and at this point I went there and poured myself a good drink. When I returned, the fire was burning again.

I had a telephone in the cabin, installed only a week before. This had been more or less a mistake, I'll admit. I had figured on using it to make a few calls of my own, and to receive a few invitations to dinner, but it had turned out mostly to be an instrument used by various merchants around town to communicate with me with respect to the fact that they were trying to put their kids through school.

It occurred to me that there was a chance to use it in a constructive way, so I called up Willie. "Now what in the hell's the matter?" he asked.

"I need a new fire extinguisher," I said.

"You haven't even used up the one you have," he said.

"That's what you think," I said.

"What did you do with it?" he enquired graciously. "Drink it?"

"What's the point in being facetious?" I said. "This is no time for joking. The cabin is on fire."

"I see," he said noncommittally.

"If you don't believe the cabin's on fire," I said, "just step outside your door in about fifteen minutes. Anything up to half an hour. Look up, and you'll see your cabin reflected on the clouds." Although I of course had opened my door and the windows, there still was so much smoke around that I had to cough. I said, "Willie, this is not a chronic cough. It's from smoke. And above all, don't forget to bring an ax."

Willie hesitated. "I'll come over," he said cautiously. "If," he added, "'you have a drink on hand."

I told him I had one, hung up, then removed my typewriter, my files, my extra clothing, and certain keepsakes from the cabin, just in case. No use taking chances. I sat down to my dinner again, but the smoke was too much and I went outside and sat on the top step to wait for Willie. After a few minutes I saw him coming past the lights cast by the Chevrolet Garage. He was walking at a good pace but not trotting, which he should have been doing. He had a fire extinguisher. No ax.

When he came up to me, in the darkness, he said, "Look, Don, a joke is a joke. If you're kidding me——"

I had my flashlight with me and I aimed a beam of light at the north face of the cabin. Some wisps of smoke, a thin compact type, the businesslike kind, white and sinister, were floating out from between the logs. "That's not mist," I said. "Not at this time of year. In the spring, maybe yes. Not now."

"The cabin's on fire," he conceded.

"Tell me some news," I said.

We went inside, where the smoke was worse than ever. With the aid of my flashlight and the candles he looked over the situation. He got up on my bed. "Hand me your ax," he said.

"What ax?" I asked gleefully. "I've been trying to get an ax from you ever since I rented the cabin. And I especially asked you to bring one with you tonight. You didn't do it. Maybe this will give you an idea of what it's like to be without an ax."

Willie didn't say anything. Some flames were showing. He aimed the new extinguisher at them, pumped it, and the thing soon was empty and there was no more flame. "Well," he said, "there goes a buck and a quarter. The fillings for these extinguishers are strictly a racket. But anyway the fire's out."

"That's what you think," I said.

We went outside to get some air. "Where's the drink?" he asked me. I told him it was on the bathroom window sill. He went into the cabin and came out with the whiskey. He was coughing. "The fire is burning again," he said, in a discouraged tone. We had a drink. "I'm going to call up the fire department," he said. "Can I use your phone?" I told him he could, under the circumstances, and he went back in. In a few minutes he came out and took another drink. "I gave the alarm," he said. "The only thing is, I don't know if they can find this cabin. You know how it is with the fire department; they enjoy a good fire as well as the next fellow; when they get a call they go around looking for a large flame. This fire we have here doesn't even show. We better start one here outside, as a guide."

I thought it over. In the cabin I had a large carton, waist high, obtained from the grocery store, that I called my Central Disposal Unit. It was close enough to my bed so that I could lie there, finish reading a newspaper or magazine and idly toss it, or drop it, with a careless flourish, into the Unit, yawning and ready for sleep. Yet standing at my stove, or sitting at my table, I easily could handle undesirable leftovers and general garbage, and grease, in the same way. When it was full I would take it outdoors and burn it up, in toto, Unit and all, and the store would give me a new one. I always was careful to distribute the grease between layers of other things, and to douse the whole thing with kerosene from a can I kept for this purpose just before burning, in order to have it burn up quickly and not smolder, on account of the garbage.

I had a piece of compoboard on hand that was larger than

the top of the Central Disposal Unit, and when I had guests I would place this over it, cover the ensemble with a tablecloth, and that was where we would dine. It worked out fine; none of my guests ever discovered they were eating on top of the garbage pail, so to speak. And it was wonderful for cleaning up things after the guests had left. Take the top off the table and scrape everything into it.

I now went into the cabin and got this and dragged it outside and poured some kerosene into it. As I was about to light it, the town fire siren sounded. This startled me; a fire siren is an eerie and frightening thing, even when there is no fire—the Jackson siren has been known to blow upon such occasions as somebody buying drinks for the house at Roy Jensen's bar, where many of the firemen gather to discuss technique.

"Light the thing," Willie said.

I applied a match to the Unit and it flared up. The first thing I saw in the light of the flame was Willie taking an extraordinarily long pull at my bottle of spirits. "Look here," I said, "just because the cabin's on fire is no reason for you drinking up all of my whiskey."

"For one thing," he said, "it's my cabin that's on fire, and I'm unhappy, I need cheering up. For another thing, who went into all that smoke to bring out the bottle?"

While I was trying to figure out a rejoinder to this, we heard the fire department coming. This certainly was surprising. Willie and I compared notes and decided that this was the fastest response either of us ever had heard of. In a short time, the main piece of equipment arrived. This was a Ford truck carrying hose, axes, fire extinguishers, and so forth. Dudley Hayden got out of the cab of the truck and came over to us.

He looked at the blazing Central Disposal Unit and he seemed a little sore. "What the hell, Don," he said, "do you mean you have broken up the square dance to have us come over here and put this thing out?"

"So that's why you got here so fast," I said. "The truck must have been parked right there."

"It was," Dudley said. "It was a good dance, Bill Jensen calling."

"I didn't know there was a dance," I said. "Nobody ever tells me anything around this town. What good is my new phone? In any case, Dudley, this isn't the main fire. This is only a decoy. The fire's inside, and getting worse." By now half a dozen firemen had parked their cars and joined us, with flashlights, and we entered the cabin. Of course there was the smoke, and now much more actual fire was showing.

"How long ago'd she start?" a fireman asked, looking at the blaze.

"Twenty minutes or so," I said. "Why?"

"Do you know what caused it?" another asked. He chuckled happily. "I always knew this cabin would burn down one of these days. An old cabin like this, she starts, and she goes."

"How about putting out the fire?" Willie asked.

"That's an idea," another fireman said. In a praiseworthy effort to spare my bed, he stepped on my table. In doing so, he aimed his flashlight at it. "What's that crap?" he asked me.

"My dinner," I said. "Look out, you're stepping on my elk steak."

"Oh, excuse me," he said. He looked the fire over, and some of the others got on my bed and helped him look it over, and they decided they needed an ax—a thing I flatter myself I could have suggested a while back, if they had asked me.

As one of them left to get the ax, Mayor Harry Clissold entered, carrying a large professional-size fire extinguisher. He took one look at the fire and got up on my bed and put it out. "It's out," he said.

"Hang around," I said.

The man who had gone for the ax brought it in and Harry took it and chopped away wallboard and charcoal right and left, then asked for another fire extinguisher, which somebody brought in. This time, as it turned out, Harry really put out the fire. Ev Mains, an electrician, now got up on my bed, which by this time looked like the city dump, and explored things with his flashlight.

"Willie," he said, "you ought to be put in jail. Do you know that you have wired this place with telephone wire?"

"What's the matter with that?" Willie asked. "If you can talk all the way from here to San Francisco over it, I don't know why it can't carry a few lights and a hotplate."

"It's not the same thing," Ev said. "If you don't know, I can't explain it. This cabin has been living on borrowed time. I'll rewire the whole place for you tomorrow."

"How much will it cost?" Willie asked.

"What difference does that make, Willie?" I said. "I didn't rent an incinerator. This time I was awake, but it could burn me up."

"Okay," Willie said.

"How was the elk steak?" Harry asked me.

"I'll never know," I said. "One of the firemen stepped on it. But never mind that. The elk steak was only partly responsible for the fire, in a very indirect way. It isn't everybody that can have a fire in his house and have the mayor of the city come over and put it out in person. I'm going to vote for you twice at the next election."

"Any support is appreciated," Harry said. "In any case, you can count on a fresh elk steak tomorrow."

Dudley Hayden and Willie drank up the rest of my whiskey, which, on my budget, was supposed to last me another week, and presently my guests left. I opened another can of corn and ate it, after throwing away my elk steak, then brought in my things from the yard. I noticed that the fire department had left a large extinguisher behind. I placed this beside my bed, having first cleaned away the debris, and eventually went to sleep.

In the morning the fire extinguisher still was there, and so was the cabin.

chapter 19

The Pause that Refreshes

WHEN winter comes, Wilford Neilson, publisher of the Jackson's Hole *Courier,** is the most popular man in town. When he walks up the street, everybody stops him and asks him how he is feeling. If he gets the sniffles, a hundred remedies are offered. If he coughs, the whole town shudders. People ask to look at his tongue, to see if it is coated.

This is not only because Wilford is a nice fellow, but because he weighs 280 pounds.

Wilford understands this concern, and he keeps telling his friends that he will do everything humanly possible not to die until spring, but every time he drinks another bottle of beer—his record is 103 in twenty-four hours—his most intimate associates can be seen counting the calories, hence the added ounces of weight, on their fingers. Through the winter months, Wilford keeps getting anonymous reducing diets in the mail.

* Jackson's Hole was named after David E. Jackson, an intrepid trapper and later a partner in the Rocky Mountain Fur Company, in 1829, when the Hole was a major crossroads of the fur trade in the West. A "hole" in Western terminology is a pocketlike valley entirely surrounded by mountains. Others in the general area were Pierre's Hole, Brown's Hole, Gardiner's Hole, and perhaps more. Jackson's Hole was the only one to escape cartographic oblivion. The designation was changed to Jackson Hole, dropping the possessive, early in the century by county officials because "The term Jackson's Hole gives rise to ribald remarks not in keeping with the dignity of this beautiful valley." The Jackson's Hole *Courier*, however, retains its original masthead and is the only source that carries the correct name of the Hole in print. All old-timers continue to pronounce it properly, of course.

When people die in Jackson, in winter, they have to be carried, by hand, part of the way to the cemetery, which is on a hillside slope at the foot of Snow King Mountain, just south of town. All but the last couple of hundred yards can be negotiated by truck, but from there on, after the snow is deep, it's strictly a muscle job.

One day Wilford and I were having a few beers over at Walt Callahan's place in Wilson, at the foot of Teton Pass.

"You'd think they'd have to carry me over the Pass," Wilford complained. "I've told them time and again that if I die between December and late April, they can quarter me. I've even put it in writing. And when the time comes—and believe me it's going to be June or July, if it kills me—I want you to put up a simple board at the head of my grave. Carve on it, 'Here Lies Wilford Neilson,' and below that, in big caps, 'THE PAUSE THAT REFRESHES.' I'll do the same for you, if you beat me to it."

We shook hands; it was a deal.

Death is a curious thing; it happens to most people, sooner or later. Look at the Civil War: out of all the tens of thousands of soldiers, only one is left. This proves, it seems to me, that it is a hard thing to avoid. Still, there is nothing funny about it. Unless you happen to die in the West, in winter, and especially if you are careless enough to freeze in a peculiar shape, in which case you automatically achieve a sort of comic immortality, this being entirely aside from what happens to your soul. (This last can be any old thing, as I understand it; I'm not taking a stand one way or the other, all I know is that in the West death can have its humorous angles, and cause many laughs, year after year. If it is bad taste for me to mention this here, then the whole West is in bad taste. The West is bigger than I am.)

Sometimes I think this approach is barbarous, but other times I think it is the most civilized thing I ever heard of.

Take the single example of a cowboy, also a top rodeo rider, who fell off a cliff up near the head of Cache Creek, and was found at the bottom, frozen stiff, all hunched up with his arms around his knees. Bill Howard found him and brought him in, without taking time to thaw him out, on the back of a pack horse. There was something about the set of the load that the horse didn't like, and every now and then he'd start bucking, and toss one of the Intermountain area's most noted bronc riders into the air and into the snow.

"That's one thing," Bill said, "that I'm glad Dee never lived to see happen."

The question of whether to try to thaw out the relict or handle him as is always is a delicate one, but Red Fenwick, in telling a story along this line in his column "Ridin' the Range" in the *Empire Magazine* of the Denver *Post* probably came across the ideal solution. It seems that a fellow by the name of Zeke died in an Idaho mining camp in midwinter and was frozen stiff when found. There were no trails open, the place was snowed in, so they unfroze him, sat him on a keg and roped him there with his legs around it, then froze him again and put him aside until toward spring. When things opened up, he was fitted to a burro and taken to town, with dignity, for his final rites.*

Jack and Ike Neal, of Jackson, met a variation of the same theme when they found a trapper frozen to death up near West Yellowstone with his arms outstretched. The Neals were traveling with a hand-pulled toboggan, on their way to Ashton, Idaho. They put the trapper on this, but their trail led through some dense stands of small lodgepole pine

* I do not vouch for this story. The only ones I swear to are my own, which I know to be true. Mr. Fenwick, a delightful columnist, is a notorious liar. Incidentally, in explaining why he was writing a column on odd deaths, Red used a line I wish I had thought of. "It seems unlikely," he wrote, "that any of us is going to get out of here alive anyhow . . ." Much better than my own feeble effort.

and the trapper's arms kept catching. In the end they were up against either chopping his arms off or melting him. Finally they built a roaring fire and softened him to the point where they could bend his arms down and lash them to his body.

Once—according to a persistent story in Jackson Hole—a cowboy got lost up on the Gros Ventre in bitter cold weather, wandered most of the night, sat down with his back to a tree to take a little rest, froze to death just below a sign on the tree that would have oriented him and saved him. But the one about the rancher who got as far as his own mailbox in a blizzard and died there, was covered with snow, and not until spring did his son find that the rock he had been stepping on all winter to open the mailbox was his missing dad, probably takes a large slice of the cake.

Fantastic as these seem, most of them either are true or have a certain element of truth in them: sometimes a lot, sometimes very little, but the general idea that death in the winter outdoors is a thoughtless way of shuffling off, imposing a burden on others, runs through them. A few years ago a chap from far up the Gros Ventre visited at the headquarters of Grand Teton National Park, and while there had a heart attack. To the dismay of everybody he disappeared a couple of days later, and it was plain that an expedition would have to make a 35-mile trek to find him.

This was done, in bitter weather; it took two or three days, but he wasn't at his cabin when they got there, and he wasn't lying dead along the trail. Upon their return he was found, frozen solid of course, in an unused privy near the headquarters building, to which he had gone because he didn't know they had a bathroom.

Stemming from these are the endless stories about words freezing in the cold, and dropping to the ground as little balls of ice, making it next to impossible to carry on a conversation. These thaw out in the spring and come to life, and a cowboy, hearing desperate calls for help, finds a man in a bear trap, dead since January. The best of these yarns, I think, is the one about the two trappers who were found frozen in their cabin for no apparent reason. They had plenty of food, there was a large pile of wood outside, there were no signs of violence. In a word, everything was in order, excepting the fact of the trappers being dead.

The discoverers of the tragedy built a fire in the stove, and as the cabin warmed up and the ice melted the last words of the doomed trappers rose from the floor. They were quarreling about whose turn it was to go out and bring in some wood.

This automatically brings us to the next subject, which will be handled in the following chapter.

chapter 20

"Everything Has a Cloudy Lining"

THINGS get a bit tough as February, that false month, edges in, grinning with one side of its face. This is when winter gets tired of itself, loses interest in life, decides nothing is worth while, rolls over and plays dead, pretending its back is broken.

Its mortal enemy, the sun, ever on the alert, watching for any toehold, happily melts the snow statues, tipping the drunken cowboy over for good, causing the skier to fall into the street and get hit by the truck and the big buck deer to lose its head. By the time winter pulls itself together and decides to try to make it through until spring (a tour de force it never has failed in, so far), just enough snow has trickled away to tease the people, who like to believe that this year, of all years, March will forget to come in with its mighty winds and its bitter cold, to bury all illusions under a million tons of fresh, unused snow.

All through the Hole, in town and out, everybody gets tired of everybody else.

Trumping your partner's ace, a shocking misdemeanor in November, now becomes a major crime; the Browning Study Club decides that Mr. Browning was, after all, a minor poet; Willard Miner tells Mr. Dews to thread his own God damn needles; housewives become convinced that the davenport would look better against the other wall; Washington and

Lincoln have their birthdays and nobody pays any attention to them, who the hell do they think they are; cowboys, feeding hay in the feed lots, kick recalcitrant steers in the pants; formerly eager merchants tell their customers to take it or leave it; a certain offbeat snarl can be heard in the song of the coyotes back in the hills and the bull elk out on the winter range look at each other with suspicion and swing their soon-to-be-shed antlers in savage farewell to their grandeur, before they all look like cows again for the summer.

Boyd Charter, one of Jackson Hole's fine cowboys, lifts his glass of beer in the RJ Bar and looks through it and says, with the convincing solemnity that somehow or other only a cowboy can manage, "At this time of year, everything has a cloudy lining."

What is all this? What is it all about? What has happened to the cocktail hour?

What has happened is cabin fever.

What is cabin fever?

Nobody knows, for sure, except that it exists.

Take the story of the two trappers up in the Wyoming hills. (If you've heard this one, stop me.) Well, they had trapped together for years, sharing a cabin, and they always were alone, never saw anybody else, for at least five months each winter. They hadn't much to say to each other; everything had been said before, so the silence in which they lived was almost as vast and deep as that of the snow and the forests by which they were surrounded.

One dull midwinter evening as they sat down to their venison stew and sourdough bannock one of them, whom we'll call Bill, said, "Saw tracks of a cow moose today."

His partner, Joe, had nothing to say at the moment, but next morning as they were starting out on their separate rounds Joe asked, in a kind of sneering way, out of the side

of his mouth, "And just how did you know it was a cow moose?"

Bill glared at him, but let it go, and they parted. That night after supper he carefully collected his personal belongings and put them into his packsack. When the packsack was full he placed it in a corner of the cabin. Joe watched, but kept his mouth shut.

In the morning, after a pleasant breakfast of coffee and pancakes and oatmeal and fried salt pork, Bill shouldered his pack. Joe watched him, then, as Bill opened the door, he asked, "What's up?"

"Pulling out," Bill said. "Too damn much argument around here to suit me." He left.

These two were suffering, of course, from a routine siege of cabin fever, a mild attack, chronic in nature as against the acute seizures that can come to the point of violence. Against this, they were using the device known as the old clam-up, a spell that Bill had broken when he mentioned having seen the tracks of a cow moose. (If it *was* a cow moose. And it certainly was, I think. A person who can't tell the tracks of a cow moose, as against those of a bull moose, in the snow, has no business in the woods. Joe probably knew this; he just would not give Bill an inch.)

This peculiar ailment, cabin fever, is unique in that it must hit its victims in pairs or not at all. One person cannot have it alone. Three persons cannot have it together. In fact, if two persons have it, and a third person shows up, nobody has it; and oddly enough, if a third person does not show up, it can be completely cured by one of the pair suffering from it simply walking away, as our friend Bill did.

I hope I have made this crystal clear.

A watered-down version of cabin fever can run through a whole settlement, but the two-man job is the real thing. It comes to trappers, forest rangers, prospectors, timber cruisers, cowboys (sheepherders never have it; there are too many people around), shipwrecked sailors, and so on. It has its roots in an unreasoning and unreasonable cumulative antipathy based on nothing that either party possibly could explain later, without looking foolish.

Whence comes the virus of this fever-that-is-no-fever? The virus, like the dreadful ailment itself, is mental, of course. This is predicated on the fact, I believe, that the human eye tends uncontrollably to follow any movement against a static background and the ear thirsts for the slightest sound in a silent world.

Suppose yourself to be alone in a closed room in which there is neither movement nor sound. You light a cigarette, and watch the smoke; a fly circles around, you watch the fly; the fly buzzes, or whatever it is that a fly does, and you listen to it; the winds sough softly through the trees outside, and you strain your ears to catch it. Now, then, if you are penned up with another person for any protracted period, he becomes the focal point of your whole being. You watch his every move, because you can't help it; every sound he makes comes in like thunder. Tiny things, without any significance whatever, are impressed upon you: the constant repetition of a simple movement, or a peculiarity of speech, or an unimportant routine personal habit, pile up in agonizing impact.

The other guy just can't do *anything* right.

He constantly clears his throat, or he never clears his throat; he always puts on his right boot first, or he always puts on his left boot first, or the idiot doesn't seem to give a damn which boot he puts on first. He wears his hat all the time indoors (or he never wears it indoors); he gurgles when he drinks his coffee (or he never gurgles when he drinks it); he puts too much sugar in his coffee (or he drinks his coffee without sugar); he blows on his oatmeal (he never blows on his oatmeal, as you do); he repeatedly hums snatches of the same stale tune (or he never hums anything); he always hangs the skillet on the wrong nail (or he always ostentatiously hangs it on the right one); he eats more than his share of the stew (while you are eating more than your share of the bannock, perhaps).

He can't win, any more than you can win.

So now the two-edged sword definitely hangs in the air. Mild irritation grows into resentment, revulsion lifts its ugly head, imagination runs wild (when the guy sharpens his skinning knife he is planning to kill you), and now comes sullen enmity, and bitterness, or worse.

The disease usually is met in one or another of three ways. The first, much preferred by old hands, is the clam-up, which I have mentioned. This is handled either in tacit understanding or through a negotiated peace: live and let live, this agony can't last forever. Sometimes a line is drawn across the floor, each one keep to his own side, and no questions asked.

The second way is that of the chronic recurrent quarrel, snarling and inconclusive. That is bad, because the nature of cabin fever is such that each patient gets angrier with the other if he doesn't quarrel, or simply won't quarrel, than if he insists on quarreling.

The third way, of course, is that of outright physical explosion, ending God-knows-where. Nobody knows how many deaths attributed to "natural causes" (such as a bullet hole in the head) or "accidents" (skull split with ax) actually represent the fatality-incident of cabin fever. The thought here is inescapable that this must be a rather frustrating form of murder, because as the loser breathes his last the cabin fever is over for both, and it's not too hard to imagine the victor, suddenly cured, standing over his victim stretched out on the cabin floor and trying his best to figure out what could have happened to such a wonderful guy . . .

One calm day in early February, the sun high, mercury nervously fluttering, barometer uncertain, tempers snapping, snow statues melting, telephone wires whispering, Wilford Neilson and Mayor Clissold got all dressed up. They washed their faces and shaved, had haircuts, put on suits of clothes, clean white shirts, neckties, and walked around the town square, their boots in blinding polish.

They had no special reason for doing this. They just did it, as a sort of spontaneous gesture, a casual effort to break the monotony, perhaps, or just to have a little fun. They had nothing up their immaculate sleeves, and when people asked them what was going on, they shrugged it off: there was nothing else to do. Within an hour, however, the town was seething, the air was so thick with rumors that it virtually was throbbing. Somebody suddenly had died, and the funeral was about to be held . . . At least a dozen couples, each one designated by name, were to be married at once, His Honor officiating . . . An unknown benefactor was throwing the most elaborate party in the history of Jackson Hole at the Elks' Club . . . John and Jess Wort, owners of the Silver Dollar Bar, had broken down and were holding open house, everything free, until midnight . . .*

And nobody knows what else; every possibility was explored.

A number of people, playing the percentages, hurried home and got into their Sunday clothes, and by late afternoon a modest crowd of newly well-dressed citizens was following Harry and Wilford wherever they went: the poor guys

* Leave us not get the idea here that the Worts never broke down and bought a drink. Each New Year's Eve there is open house, all free, from four until six in the afternoon. Vern Hess, the town baker, once stopped in for a Tom & Jerry during this delightful interlude and told Willard Miner, after sipping it, "This drink is too God damn sweet." "Look," Willard said, "it's on the house. You got any more complaints?" Vern shut up and drank his drink, and a few more. Sharply at six the free-loading was off, and Vern ordered another, placing a dollar on the bar. He sipped it. "Willard," he said, "this drink is too God damn sweet."

couldn't even visit a gentlemen's retiring room without a claque at their heels.

By dusk the whole town was dressed up. Still meeting all questions with the equivalent of the Republican platform, "No comment," our heroes dined at a window table in Jack Moore's Open Range Café, eating huge steaks and smoking expensive cigars. Jack had his best day of the year, his place jammed with distinguished-looking guests and others waiting to get in. Then, the mounting tension becoming next to unbearable, Harry and Wilford, still followed by bitter-enders, went home, got into something comfortable, and called it a day.

This casual afternoon stroll, as it turned out, took its place right up there beside the midnight ride of Paul Revere, Sherman's march from Atlanta to the sea, the flight of the Wright brothers at Kitty Hawk, the travels of Marco Polo, and Fred Merkle's uncompleted run to second base in the ninth inning of the Cub-Giant game of September 9, 1908, at the Polo Grounds.

In a word, it was historic.

Perhaps it was not historic within any recognized major area of human endeavor, such as war and flying and peaceful coexistence on the international level, or baseball, but it marked a turning point in the history and culture of Jackson Hole, which is as much a part of the world as anyplace else.

The Clissold-Neilson contribution, however, was indirect in terms of practical application. Neither one of these scientists claimed either to have isolated the cabin-fever virus or to have produced an effective vaccine, by putting on a clean shirt and a $1.25 necktie and reserving comment. This would have been a bit too close to Dr. Coué, Mother's Day, and Rotary International. The people of Jackson Hole wear boots, but no bootstraps; they do not subscribe to the theory that a woman can solve all her troubles, either in real life or over the radio, by going out and buying a new hat, or that a man can become chairman of the board of General Motors by nodding his head 64,000 times.

Jackson, triggered by the C-N formula while still rejecting it as the answer, with characteristic directness went straight to the roots of cabin fever for inspiration and guidance. Merely dressing up, supposing one person's shirt to be a shade cleaner than that of his neighbor, or his tie of a color likely to set the grocer's teeth on edge, easily could add to, not break up, the pattern of the disease, compounding everything. On the other hand, the arrival of a third party, or the emergence of any outside distraction or interest, always whipped it in no time at all.

Therefore, in hitting on the idea of a winter carnival, complete with a lovely queen to sit upon a throne of ice (a suggestion vigorously opposed by Mr. Dews, who felt that in view of the general situation it ought to be an electric blanket), along with various ceremonies, races, square-dancing, contests, and a great elk-meat supper to finish it off—early-morning drinking to be included—the objective aimed at was to induce people from other places to visit Jackson, for the occasion. People from other towns, other states, other countries, other hemispheres, other planets, other everything.

"We're too much alone here in winter," Mayor Clissold said in a semiofficial proclamation. "We need new blood, fresh faces, friendship, neighborliness with our neighbors, a spirit of cooperation, a mixing up of people. Also," he added, moving his fingers in a vague gesture, "we need more money."

Although a few of the sterner citizens were a bit hesitant about the suggestion of "a mixing up of people," which they thought there was enough of already without aid from strangers, the plan itself enthusiastically was received, and implementation began at once. After several bitter quarrels it was decided to send a cavalcade of motorcars over into Idaho, down to Utah as far as Salt Lake City, over into southern Wyoming, and back to Jackson. More than twenty cars were assembled. Each car was decorated with a banner, some of which were painted by two of the West's finest artists, Archie Teator and Conrad Schwiering, both long-time residents of Jackson.*

The legends included such persuasive ones as HOWDY, PARDNER!; WELCOME TO JACKSON HOLE!; COME ONE, COME ALL!; SEE THE WORLD'S LARGEST ELK HERD!; ALL ROADS ALWAYS OPEN!; RACES, GAMES, FUN!; THE LAST OF THE OLD WEST! (This one—THE LAST OF THE OLD WEST!—was an especially fancy job, mounted rigidly on the top of Roy Jensen's new Cadillac, which, as though in symbol, brought up the rear of the procession.)

The automobiles circled the town square of Jackson, and paraded elsewhere through the streets, horns wide open as the citizenry cheered, then unwound itself and hit the trail.

This start of the great cavalcade was the signal for the garrison instantly to turn to the work at hand. The election of the Queen, it was decided, should come first. A great throne of ice blocks (Mr. Dews still dissenting) was set up in the middle of the park, and properly floodlighted and further decorated with colored bulbs, courtesy of the elec-

* Archie Teator, originally a cowboy and trapper, in 1952 had a section of the late supersophisticated *Flair* magazine devoted to himself and to his work, and has had two one-man shows in the exclusive galleries of 57th Street, New York. He never studied art formally, but for years waded deep in icy water in Jackson Hole, tending his beaver traps, in order to buy time for painting, which I suppose is a kind of formal education after all. He paints in a style entirely his own, with accentuation on figures, and scenes involving figures, all local and anecdotal in approach. Connie Schwiering, on the other hand, is a student of, and instructor in, the traditional depiction of mountain scenery, with a realistic, almost photographic, attention to color, mass, and detail. He has gained many honors for his expert work, and his highly decorative paintings always are in demand, both nationally and in the local tourist area.

tric company, and now, the target set, the voting began.

The voting was by ballots printed in the *Courier*, distributed in the business establishments, and otherwise made available. The participation of the voters was gay, uninhibited, good-natured, unfair, and crooked. Then when the contest narrowed down to a pretty telephone operator, a reticent, home-loving girl, devoted to her mother and to the Baptist church, and a magnificent cocktail waitress who had been stranded in town for the winter, the whole thing became serious and proceeded strictly along party lines.

The telephone operator won by a beautiful nose, and the Republicans proclaimed a new era in Jackson, the start of another crusade.

In other directions, things went along smoothly. The skiers who were to come down the side of Snow King Mountain, at the edge of town, in a slow slalom the night of the Coronation, each carrying a torch made of rags soaked in kerosene, made practice runs. The various ladies' clubs made preparations for the elk-meat supper to be held not only in the Elks Hall but in other places for the overflow crowds; spare rooms were made ready for paying guests; the merchants arranged displays of their best stocks and sent out emergency orders to Idaho Falls; the restaurants squeezed in extra tables; the bank postponed notes due.

The bars brought reserve cases from their cellars, the square-dance callers practiced their art, the kids ran trial heats with their dog sleds, the cutter racers thundered through town, the gas station owners filled their tanks, the gamblers flexed their fingers, rubbing and loosening them to be sure they were quicker than the eye, and shuffled and reshuffled their cards, to be on the safe side.

A great WELCOME! sign was erected.

Meantime, news from the cavalcade was pouring in. Success was topping success. Driggs! Ashton! Idaho Falls! Pocatello! Ogden! Salt Lake! Then later Evanston, Kemmerer,

Rock Springs, Pinedale, and all way stops and way stations. Reception committees, mayors, the governor, the newspapers, civic organizations—breakfasts, luncheons, dinners, parades, speeches, more parades . . .

The great cavalcade arrived home in full cry, battle flags somewhat tattered by foreign winds—and perhaps by arrows, for they had gone through Indian country—but with spirit undiminished. Everybody gathered in the square, and now here is Dictator Clissold, his arm upraised for quiet, addressing his loyal subjects:

"The trip has been a tremendous success, and our winter festival will draw thousands . . . However, the best thing of all is getting home. You have to meet a lot of people in order to understand and appreciate your own neighbors, whether they are the ones with you on the trip or those you return to . . . In the end it may well be that we'll find this more important than anything else . . ."

As it turned out, this was one of His Honor's most important speeches. All great leaders must have a sense of history, must be able to project themselves into the future and from that vantage point look back upon, and evaluate, what they are doing, and what they are saying, at the moment. This gift, in a word, is the exact opposite of second guessing. It is first guessing, in the highest degree.

Did Harry Clissold *know* that a great storm was coming, or did he just make a wonderful guess?

Nobody knew at the time, and nobody has known since, for Harry has clammed up.

In any case, reports now began to come in from the outside.

The snow was drifting heavily in Idaho, where roads were closing and train schedules were off . . . The storm was sweeping Utah, too . . . The road from Rock Springs to Pinedale, across the Little Colorado desert, a distance of ninety miles, was just about hopeless . . . Highway departments were warning against all but emergency travel.

At first the festival was postponed for a few days only, but when Slide Number One ran on Teton Pass and not even the mail could make it through Hoback Canyon, everybody knew it was hopeless. Jackson waited until the wind went down and the snow let up, then held its winter festivity, alone.

It was a wonderful thing, a happy time.

One reason for this was that it got off on the right foot, in the proper spirit, when the people began to discover, in a surge of unseasonable frankness among themselves, that nobody really gave a damn whether any visitors came or not. The cavalcaders had included about one out of every nine of the total population, and they certainly had had it: just as Mayor Clissold said, the more they saw of other people during the trip the happier they were to huddle together by themselves at the time, then to get home. Privacy, the general idea seemed to be, was a God-given thing. And now they had it.

The cutter races were thrilling; the kids' dog races, although inconclusive, were packed with action; the skiers came down the side of the mountain with their torches, in an unusual spectacle; the square-dancing came off with very few actual fights. The great elk dinner was splendid. With no outsiders to mess things up, friends of precabin-fever days became friends all over again. A lady who had been on an almost nonspeaking basis with me since the great snow-statue contest insisted on filling my plate twice, and with the choicest cuts. The hall sang with light conversation and there was laughter in the air, and good-fellowship—and not a foreigner in town.

The crowning of the Queen was touching and memorable, a graceful thing here in this tiny settlement so far from all others, under the shadow of the towering Tetons, and the hush of the deep snow seemed appropriate. The Queen herself, in her beautiful robe and her tinsel tiara, was lovely.

So far as the merchants and the restaurants and bars were concerned, everything came out fine. The people dug into their socks, in this festive air, and found a few spare quarters to spend where they chose.

"Now I tell you," Mr. Dews said, sipping his breakfast in the Silver Dollar, "it's easy to get in a rut where you think the best things ought to be for other people; they are too good for you. I remember when I was a kid, what we had to eat was divided into two classes, what was good enough for company and what was good enough for us. When Father would bring home something especially good, Mother would say, 'My goodness, that's almost nice enough for company.' She would bake up a batch of cookies, in case company came in, and we dasn't touch them. When we would have what she called a 'company dinner' all by ourselves it made her nervous; she seemed to think we were cheating other people out of it. One Sunday we had a lovely fat chicken, and she said something about it's being good enough for company and Father struck the table with his fist. 'We are just as good as anybody who comes to see us!' he shouted. 'Our kids are company! Nothing that we can afford to buy and pay for is too good for us!'

"Well," Mr. Dews continued, "that's the way I feel about things around here right now. I don't take much part in it, I have my own duties to perform, but I think it's nice. 'God bless us, one and all.' Who said that?"

"Tiny Tim, I think," I said.

"I don't know," Mr. Dews said. "I remember it from school. I thought it was Admiral Perry."

I have nothing to add to what Mr. Dews had to say.

chapter 21

Social Notes (March)

The Goldfish

ABOUT half the population of the town of Jackson is made up of persons, or the relict thereof, who dropped in by accident or happened along for reasons having nothing to do with any intention of permanent residence—hunters, for example, or in earlier days armed individuals other than hunters —but who either stayed on at the time because they wanted to, or had to, or else returned later to take up serious citizenship.

Among these last was Jon Stainbrook, who owns the Jackson Variety Store. He was a college-boy bus driver in Yellowstone Park and came down into the Hole in the line of duty one day in 1935 and looked it over and decided to come back. He made it a few years later, loaded with an idea for raising trout in a series of ponds. This didn't work, but he was determined to stay. He read someplace that you could buy a "package" of merchandise for setting up a variety store, so he sent for one and rented a little vacant space and was in business.

Today he has the largest mercantile establishment in Jackson Hole, with more than 14,000 items of merchandise, not any one of which he can find. He lets the customers do it. His special profits come from selling to tourists things he had had shipped in, over Teton Pass, from their own home towns, and that they could have bought back there at a considerable, sometimes a sensational, saving. "Found it in a messed-up little store high in the Wyoming mountains," they tell their friends. "The poor fellow couldn't have known its real value." (The poor fellow is not quite a millionare yet, but he ain't doing no complaining.) *

A few years ago when cabin fever went into its inevitable March recurrence—you think you have it licked in February, then go into a decline in March, the month everybody forgets about—Jon thought of a way in which he might be of service to the community, above and beyond the call of duty. He never quite had got over his old idea of raising trout; the collapse of that venture, due to the overlong winters, still rankled. Now, going back in a sense to his old love, he sent outside, I think to Salt Lake City, for eight hundred goldfish, assorted sizes, shapes, and coloring. They were brought in, in a large glass tank, by a heated truck, and Jon put them in his window. He had a little net for dipping them out, and a lot of small cartons in which they could be carried home and put into glass jars or other improvised aquariums.

The thing was a sensation.

Something completely new had come to town; the people dropped their quarrels and forgot their worries; they stood in subzero weather and looked at the little fish through the window, and a line of eager customers soon formed inside the store. (Including me; I bought six for my cabin; they later were to die, one by one, in spite of all I could do, but they were pleasant friends while they lived.)

By closing time Jon had sold more than three hundred fish.

* The Variety Store, although still called that by Jackson people, now is designated as The Jackson Trading Company and is known to the tougher-minded tourists as The Trading Post. By this simple change in name Jon increased his gross business by some 20 per cent, overnight, because the hardy adventurers from New York now could add to the conversation-piece value of their purchases by explaining they had bought them from an Indian.

During the night a terrible thing happened. One of the panes of the window fell out. It didn't break, it just slipped down to the floor. Jon figured later that some small fry, perhaps pressing their mittens against it from the outside, had loosened it.

In the morning the tank was a solid chunk of ice and its glass of course was broken, to boot. Jon cleared away the wreckage and took the ice, in which were embedded several hundred dead fish, out into the back yard. That was that. Cabin fever surged back as those who had fish upstaged those who did not have any. Then somebody, I don't know who it was, happened to see the big block of ice full of frozen fish out in the back yard. He certainly was an ichthyologist of the first water. He went into the hardware store next door and commandeered two or three washtubs. He cut the big chunk of fish-infested ice into small pieces and put these into the tubs, then filled the tubs with water.

The ice melted, and the fish came to life.*

Jon sold all of the fish, the people of Jackson were happy, he sent to Salt Lake for more, sold these out, and March was

* Freezing does not kill fish so long as they are fully alive when frozen, and so long as the freezing comes quickly. A friend of mine, Al Evans, once went fishing for sunfish through the ice of White Bear Lake, near St. Paul, Minnesota. It was bitter cold and the sunnies all froze solid as soon as they were out of water. When Al got home he put his catch in the bathtub and drew some water to thaw them so he could clean them for supper. He himself was pretty well chilled, so he took a few drinks against the possibility of pneumonia. When he went to the bathtub to get his fish they were swimming around in gay fashion, evidently looking for the soap so they could take a bath, and Al went on the wagon and stayed on it for nearly ten years.

On the other hand, a slight overdose of heat can be permanently fatal. In 1931 Berry and I lived in the upstairs half of a duplex house at 626 Arlington Place, Chicago. Our landlord, Paul Fleming, who lived downstairs, had a small concrete pool in his yard just below our kitchen window. In this were eight or ten large goldfish. One day our maid, Signe Gustafsson, lately from Sweden, was broiling some lambchops, when they caught on fire. She threw the blazing chops, grid and all, out the window. The ensemble landed in the pool. All the fish quickly died. We bought new lambchops, and, later, new goldfish.

clean beat. It's hard to have cabin fever with a few beautiful fish swimming around on your window sill, especially if you got them through a first-class miracle.

The Poacher

Ed Benson for years enjoyed the most unique fishing in Jackson Hole, or anyplace else, that I know of. He caught trout all winter, no matter what the temperature, and while sitting in an easy chair in his own home. Ed brought electricity to the Hole, back in 1921. He had come in from Philadelphia in 1919 to hunt big game, was so entranced with the country that he returned the next year and decided to stay. The town needed electricity, and he undertook to furnish it. He built a log house straddling a branch of Cache Creek. The electric plant, consisting of a diesel engine and two small turbines, was set up in the basement of the house. Cache Creek ran the turbines. Ed built a small concrete pool in the basement, for technical reasons. The trout of Cache Creek liked this pool, over which Ed had hung a light, and the Bensons had trout all winter, helping out the food budget and surprising guests.

This eventually came to the notice of the Game and Fish Department, State of Wyoming. Ed's house was a private home, but these were public trout. Was he, or was he not, breaking the law by catching them out of season? This fine point was argued, out of court, between Ed and the State for quite a while, and of course the citizens of Jackson, as usual, chose up sides. It wasn't the most important thing in the world, but it was better than cabin fever.

Ed challenged the State to keep their silly trout out of his basement. They constituted a threat to his turbines, he said, and he had to catch them in self-defense.

He later cut a hole in the floor of his kitchen, above the basement pool, and used a longer fishing line. That saved him the trouble of going to the basement for his fish, and they came to the kitchen ice cold and wiggling. He now told the State that it was up to them to keep their confounded fish out of his kitchen, citing the fact as an invasion of his privacy.

Nobody could find an answer to that one, and the matter was dropped.

Ed had his struggles in the early days of his electric plant. He had six customers the first year and fifteen the second year, but ended in 1952, when he sold his holdings to the Government, with seven hundred. When he started his little under-the-house plant on Cache Creek he had to dam the creek to form a large pond, covering several acres, to give force to the flow through his turbines. The excess water ran free through a spillway outside of the house. When the pond froze, Ed put a few electric lights over it, by way of advertising and as a community service, and invited the kids of the town to skate there.

It became a popular place.

As everybody else had to, he spent a lot of time cutting firewood, which he carefully piled beside the pond. This wood never seemed to last as long as it should have, and Ed couldn't figure it out. One cold night he noticed a couple of young skaters gleefully throwing chunks of the wood into the part of the creek that bypassed his house.

"Boys, boys!" he said. "My goodness, that's no way to do! Don't you realize that cutting that wood represents a lot of work?"

"Yes, sir," the boys said politely.

"Then you musn't waste it like that," Ed said.

The boys seemed relieved. "Oh, we're not wasting it, Mr. Benson," one of them said. "Our pa and our older brother are downstream a ways, taking it out of the creek and stacking it beside our house."

Breathless Love

By no means the least of the urges engendered in the people of Jackson Hole by the impact of their surroundings, and brought to special fruition during the semi-isolation of the snow, with emphasis on March, is the urge to write. Shoot an arrow into the winter air and later you will find it embedded in the breast of a person who is working on Page One of Chapter Three.

Frenchy, in his remote Buffalo Fork cabin, comes in from his trap line and after skinning his beaver perhaps tries to stay awake long enough to put in some work on his book about the Brooklyn Dodgers, just as Owen Wister, in his cabin across the valley, many years ago wrote that immortal tale of the West, *The Virginian,* the scene of which was Jackson Hole; and Joe Jones, in the shed behind his grocery store, contributed what he could.

The old-timer wishes to tell tales of the early days when things were tough all over, and history was made, not merely written; the newcomers, relatively speaking, feel the drama around them, and of which they are a part, for Jackson Hole is drama incarnate, and they sharpen their pencils and get to work. I conducted a discussion group in the winter of 1949–50 in the lobby of the Wort Hotel, by means of which I tried to pass on to some of these colleagues a few of the practical, or trade, aspects of this endeavor, with which they were not familiar but that I had learned over the years. These people came in through some of the damnedest weather you ever saw, often for miles, to take part in the discussions. Here I am speaking of their own intensity, not of anything of any real value that I had to offer. I was the hitching post.

Another incentive toward implementation of this urge to write is the fact that this fits in with a tradition in Jackson

Hole. Struthers Burt, one of the country's foremost novelists until his death in 1953, was a pioneer rancher here, later started the Hole's first dude ranch, the BAR BC. He was living at his lovely ranch on Pacific Creek when he was stricken, and there his wife, Katharine Newlin Burt, for years an outstanding writer for top magazines and author of some memorable novels, still lives. Olaus Murie, who with his wife Mardy lives a few miles north of Jackson, is one of the country's top writers and most respected authorities on natural history and wilderness ecology subjects. Frances Judge (hostess at the tragic Christmas Eve party when Sunny Allan wrecked the works with his roller-skate snowshoes) is nationally known for her fine stories, all stemming from her experience here, and Grace Nelson, Almer's wife, has a wide following with her gracious and friendly interpretation of the wild life of the valley.

However, it was left to Bill Howard, that wonderful cowboy, to come through with the greatest writing effort of modern times, if not of all history.*

Bill had got tired of being a cowboy because he always was wet, cold, and hungry. "Show me a cowboy who isn't wet, cold, and hungry," he once said, "and I'll show you a bum cowboy. He's got to be wet, cold, and hungry all the time, not just once in a while."

So one day he decided to get in out of the rain and write a book, then retire. "There isn't one single word in any of

* I was very fond of Bill, we always had fun, in spite of his having once stolen a pair of expensive binoculars from me. I had these Zeiss glasses but was out of money and I pawned them to Bill for eight dollars. Soon after that, while Bill was back in the hills, I left for California. I sent him a check for eight dollars and asked him to send on the glasses. No response, and the check never was cashed. Over a period of three years I did the same thing several times. No answer. After nine years I returned to the Hole, and there was Bill, in the Silver Dollar. "Where the hell are my glasses?" I asked him. "I don't know," he said. "I didn't send them to you because you were out there in California, and I figured I needed them worse than you did. Have a drink?" And that was the end of *that* subject.

these books that isn't in the dictionary," he declared. "All I need is a dictionary."

He found one in the Jackson library, bought some pencils and pads of paper, and got down to work. First he wrote out the title, *Breathless Love,* then started reading the dictionary. After two weeks of hard labor he had two pages of *Breathless Love* finished. He quit.

I don't suppose Bill ever would have been a successful writer, but he sure as hell had a title, didn't he? Perhaps if he had just pasted the title to the dictionary and sent the whole thing to Hollywood, he might have died rich. As it was, he died just a fine cowboy. When, a year later, he was stricken with a heart attack and I got a telegram from Jackson—I was in New York at the time—that read BREATHLESS LOVE IS DEAD, I knew what it meant.

The Joiners-Up

The people of Jackson Hole, especially those living in Jackson, have a passion for keeping up with the rest of the world, not only by having turkey at Thanksgiving but in every other way possible. This is particularly true, of course, during the winter months, when at times it is much easier to keep up with the rest of the world than it is to keep up with Jackson itself. Red Cross drives, the March of Dimes, the Community Chest, campaigns for the control of cancer, it doesn't matter what it is, anything on a national or even state-wide basis finds Jackson on its toes for a major effort, and the town and the Hole never yet have failed to more than meet their obligations.

Some of these endeavors, such as obeying the blackout rules for Western states during World War II in order to guard against attack by enemy aircraft, may seem a bit ambitious to the casual observer, who does not understand the therapeutical aspects of much of this activity, calculated to keep everybody from going nuts. During the World War II blackouts and dimouts and brownouts, all hands following the rules, hour by hour, Wilford Neilson noted in his paper, "Many of us feel that this is unnecessary, but it has a very real value in giving us a sense of participation in, and an understanding of, what other places, in more danger of immediate attack than we are, have to do."

The materialization of the atomic bomb in Russia had its effect on the community and social life of Jackson. The following is quoted from the February, 1951, issue of the *Courier*:

> **Civil Defense Is Topic of Next Meeting of Legion and Auxiliary, February 6**
>
> The next meeting of the American Legion and Auxiliary, to be held February 6 at the Legion home, will be devoted to a discussion of civil defense. Ken Reimers will talk on survival in case of atomic attack, and Dr. Elmore is scheduled to talk on this subject, and the warning signs to be used. Other matters pertinent to the subject will be discussed. The meeting will be a joint one, and any who are not members yet are interested in the subject are invited to attend.

At present Jackson not only has an active Civil Defense unit, but is doing its part in the national aircraft-spotting program, watching for suspicious planes.

Jackson not only has chapters or lodges of the usual organizations, such as the Legion, VFW, Odd Fellows, Elks, Kiwanis, Rotary, and so on, but in 1953 set up its own chapter, or whatever it is called, of Alcoholics Anonymous.

The money collected, mostly at the bars, in those tin cans I have mentioned, for putting up a place in town that would keep the kids away from the dangers of the countryside, was not quite enough for the purpose, so it was added to a privately organized fund for erecting a ski shelter at the foot of Snow

King Mountain, half a mile south of town. There is a great skiing layout on the mountainside, and a chair lift for taking people to the top.

The shelter was the only place in town where a fellow could get warm without buying a drink, and for some reason or other this Alcoholics Anonymous chapter was formed, to meet there every two weeks. Since notices of each meeting are run in the *Courier* and in Floy Tonkin's Jackson Hole *Guide,* this is probably the least anonymous of any AA group in the world.

It also has the distinction of having had its meeting place erected largely with money collected in the bars, for another purpose, which quite naturally leaves the bars wondering what the hell.

Tragedy on a Hillside

A major means of personal transportation in Jackson Hole is the ski. The native ski is about twelve feet long, nearly a foot wide, and is propelled, or guided, through a built-on housing made of heavy leather and nailed to the ski itself. It has no hinge action. It is large enough so that the skier can put not only his foot into it, but whatever he is wearing: moccasins, shoes, boots, overshoes. The leather extends up to just above ankle height, and sewed to this is an extension made of canvas, going on to the knee, where it lightly is tied with a piece of string. The canvas keeps the snow away from the housing, but in case of trouble the string will break and let the skier fall free. (The working cowboy always ties the two legs of his chaps together with string for much the same reason: he doesn't want leather thongs, or a buckle, to hook over the horn of the saddle in an emergency and hang him up there. He wants a breakaway.)

These skis usually have a long strip of elk hide set into the working surface, with the hairs pointed toward the rear.

This keeps the ski from back-slipping when the traveler is going uphill, while still letting him glide downhill without slowing him up too much. In going downhill he does not slalom, but, as I think the expression is, schlusses. Goes straight ahead. He has a stout pole about as long as his skis, and if he gets to going too fast he puts this between his legs and sits on it, using it as a brake. After all, the man is at work. He is skiing because he has to, not because he wants to, accepting the ski just as he accepts a horse: strictly a nuisance, but if you've got to go you've got to go.

Now, for no reason penetrable by the normal mind, a certain number of people began coming into the Hole for the purpose—or what appeared to be the nonpurpose—of going all the way to the top of a hill and sliding all the way down again, on their skis. Then doing it all over. At the end of the day they ended precisely at the point from which they had started.

Their skis were short, narrow, equipped with a highly flexible harness. They carried two dainty bamboo poles, one in each hand, which they used as wands, and they came downhill in balletlike swings and dances, like so many Rockettes from the Radio City Music Hall in New York City. In a word, they seemed to be going to all this trouble just for fun. Some of the local people got the idea, or pretended to, and became devotees of this incredible ritual. They fashioned the ski run down Snow King Mountain with the help of the United States Forest Service, put up the Ski Shelter, organized a ski lift to take people to the top of the hill without effort on their part.

Naturally, there were many arguments about whether these fancier skiers could get from the top to the bottom of the hill, with their racing equipment, faster than could the working skier, with his clumsy outfit. By this time some very important skiers from outside were coming in to the Hole—among them Andrea Mead, who won the Olympic championship in 1955.

So a contest was arranged. Six fancy skiers and six local skiers, using the traditional ski that I have described, all were to start from the top of the mountain at the same time, and let the best man get to the bottom first. The odds heavily favored the sports skier, in the betting.

Came the big day.

All twelve skiers started at once. The ballet dancers began their incredibly swift and graceful sweeps, from side to side. The local boys came straight down, sitting well back on their poles, when necessary. One of these, taking a bump head on, lost a ski. It sailed on ahead of him, the leather housing of course still attached to it, and the canvas flapping.

"My God!" a spectator cried. "He's lost a leg!"

An instant later another local boy lost both skis at once.

"He's lost both legs!" a lady from foreign parts shrieked and, according to eyewitnesses, fainted.

The result? An exact tie. There was too much snow flying through the air at the finish line to be sure. At the very last moment, with an elk-hide skier ahead, sure to win, one of the opposition took a dangerous short cut and both fell across the line together.

Tragedy in a Washing Machine

All these various gadgets that come into the Hole—electricity, automobiles, the telephone, streamlined skis, radio, canned beer, automatic pencils, turkeys, Civil Defense, and God knows what next—undoubtedly have their place in the general scheme of things, but some of them have their own built-in hurdles, too.

John Dodge had cooked string beans for thirty-five years, tender and nice as could be, before he had to have a pressure cooker blow up and nearly kill him, and Farney Cole had washed his clothes in the creek for a long, long time before he had to meet his Armageddon in a bowl of synthetic suds guaranteed not to roughen the most tender skin. Farney, an old-time cowboy, got a job as winter caretaker of a summer home up on Flat Creek. Among other things that he came across was an electric washing machine. He had some personal clothing that could stand plenty of soap and water, after a summer in the Gros Ventre hills. He read the instructions carefully, then filled the machine with his washable clothes, water, and some soap powder.

According to the instructions, which featured a picture of a happy housewife playing tennis while Westinghouse did the dirty work, he now could turn the thing on and forget it. This is exactly what he did.

The engine of the jeep needed some attention, and he figured he would have plenty of time to drive into town and have this handled, instead of playing tennis. He drove in, and left the jeep at the garage, then strolled over to the Log Cabin and had himself a beer. He met some colleagues.

"All this time," he told them, "my clothes are being washed, automatically. Good Christ, what an age we live in!"

Farney Cole was a mighty popular guy, and he had many friends, and he hadn't been to town for a long time . . .

Two days later, on his way back to the ranch with his jeep, he remembered the washing machine. He felt a bit uneasy, but realized that if the thing was adjusted to shut itself off at the end of a set or two of tennis there was nothing to worry about, and if it was not, there no longer was anything to worry about, either.

When he got there, the monster still was going, and all that was left of his clothes was an incredible mishmash of threads, buttons, and a couple of zippers.

He took the loss of his clothes in good spirit; it all was soapsuds over the dam, no hard feelings. Only one thing bothered him, and it kept bothering him more and more as the winter wore on.

He came into town now and then, for a shot or two of Crème de Menthe. He would shake his head, frowning. "What the hell," he kept saying, "there was at least a half pint of little buttons in that thing that I never saw before in my life."

Part 4. AH, SPRING!

chapter 22

The Back Yard Springs to Life

ONE FINE morning in late April, 1939, Berry came into our Jackson house, her cheeks rosy from the sharp moist air of spring, and stomped the particles of rotten snow, half snow and half ice in heavy granules, from her overshoes.

"The garden's going to be lovely this year," she said. "It looks very much like a bumper crop."

I waited, apprehensively, for she spoke in a dulcet tone that struck terror to my heart.

"Yes?" I said.

"Yes," she said. "Four more whiskey bottles are up through the snow this morning, and two new rums are breaking the surface, just showing their cunning little necks. And the beer patch continues to emerge beautifully."

Ah, Spring, Alas!

People who live in large cities know little about this season of the stirring of new life beyond what they read in the newspapers: the urban spring reflects mostly the traditional direction taken by the flight of a young man's fancy . . . Farmers are hep to spring because they're in the business. But those it hits hardest are the small-towners, and to them it is a terrible thing to have to go through.

With emphasis on the male element (as I may have indicated) it's the season of apprehension, even of fear, of self-search and perhaps of guilt, for while the city people enjoy the new crop of park benches and the farmers burst from the confinement of winter like willow buds along the streams and look forward to still another gamble with drought and parity, the townspeople are faced only by the desolation of the back yard with its progressive revelation of things past.

For it is there, as the snow recedes, that the wreckage of your life from November on, in its whole ugly pattern, unfolds before your eyes—and before those of your wife—in slow motion, just as those trick movie cameras show flowers of a somewhat different stripe upfolding to the urge of the morning sun.

Naturally you start off in the fall with a rusty steel barrel as a repository for noninflammable discards, the theory being that the local Department of Sanitation (or rough equivalent) will show up just about the time the barrel is full and the overflow is spreading. This works fine once or twice, mostly once, but then comes the first blanket of snow, covering everything up, and the department sees no need for its services and goes deer hunting. Subsequent snows repeat the purge just as things begin to look ratty again, and the department and his wife, according to the local paper, are visiting relatives in Long Beach, California.

By January the trash barrel is no more than a target, a thing loosely to aim at, hoping for the best: you just open the door a little and fire away without bothering to put on your shoes. If you hit the side of the barrel it's a bull's-eye, but if you don't hit it there's no harm done. By Washington's Birthday you don't even aim at the barrel, you just aim at the night, which is hard to miss.

This is just plain common sense. On the practical side, everything that is subject to freezing freezes solid as soon as it's thrown into the back yard, solving all problems in that direction. Looking at the aesthetic angle, the entire household discard either sinks unobtrusively into the snow then present or, in the event of these various things piling up to the point of the top layer showing, it's a cinch there will be fresh snow in a day or two.

This is a fine arrangement while it lasts: until, that is, it goes into reverse. Then, as I have suggested, there is hell to pay. The movement as a whole naturally is uneven. In an uncontaminated area (small) the bare ground itself may show, while at its edge a piece of elk hide tops a plateau two feet high, held up like some kind of magic carpet by the snow it has prevented the sun from reaching; and this, with similar vagaries, gives the scene a feeling of having been designed by Mr. Salvador Dali. For instance, the main pile, the one within easy tossing distance of the back door, stands in exposed strata, in cross section, that is, the record of the winter's snowfalls alternating with various domestic phenomena, a condensed history from the first freeze up to now.

There is Thanksgiving, nearly six inches thick, heavily laced with the bones of a bird and other symbols of a distressingly temporary plethora. Then, after evidence of a few snowfalls—relieved by a few thin strata of discarded hash, some of it burned—comes Christmas, with a layer of tinsel winking brightly at the victorious sun. After this a few bottles, representing New Year's, with memories of some delightful guests, followed by a thick outcropping of soup cans, then a lot of plain snow until February comes through with nostalgic remnants of a saddle of venison and some elk, courtesy of Mayor Clissold. Then an early-spring layer of trout bones, more snow, some ashes, and a blank.

Of course during his first winter a person is liable to make mistakes, such as throwing all his bottles into his own back yard, but presently he learns the usual tricks, mostly by having them practiced on him first. I had to have a good many bottles thrown into my yard, adding to my springtime bewilderment, before I got the idea: it's a pretty listless community in which, come the night of the Big Blizzard, the citizens aren't out heaving the evidence in all directions . . .

Once, in Jackson, I lived next door to a man who was an accomplished solitary tippler, a fact known to nearly everybody but his wife: she was aware of his tossing a few off in casual toasts to births, deaths, anniversaries, illnesses, graduations, engagements, automobile accidents and other special occasions as reported in the newspaper, and there always was a partly consumed bottle in plain sight, ostentatiously collecting dust, but she never found out about the more transient and expendable ones that were cached in the chinks between the logs and in the bottom of the soiled-clothes basket.

That winter my neighbor was favoring gin, a potion I can take only in moderate doses, while in a modest way I was enjoying a light whiskey diet. Since I wasn't sure that my wife would look at my diet as being as light as I considered it to be, I held out three of every five empties and hid them, waiting for a snowstorm. During the storm I would throw these, in the dead of night, over the fence.

I seemed in the clear, but when spring came our back yard grew a crop of gin bottles that would have warmed the heart of the Secretary of Agriculture. I had a few bad moments, trying to collect my wits, but in the end escaped unscathed because Berry well knew that I was not drinking gin. My neighbor, I found later when we got together and discovered our incredible luck, had won out on approximately the same basis: he had taken to gin because whiskey, in some sort of allergic reaction, caused him to break out under the armpits. All he had to do was to show his wife his armpits, and he was in the clear.

We shook hands on it.

That spring following the winter I put in alone in the cabin I rented from Willie Kuhrtz was the worst one I had to go through, in this respect. Berry was in the East; she was to come out along in May. So all winter I was on my own, my Central Disposal Unit working like a charm, not a worry in the world. By May, I figured, the Department of Sanitation would be back from Long Beach, the yard would be cleaned up, and I might even have a bed of pansies between my door and Pat Patterson's croquet court to welcome her.

My fault lay in my overconfidence—and my failure to remember that women sometimes change their minds. Instead of tending to business, watching that back yard like a hawk, I spent too much time writing to Berry explaining the austerity of my regimen: plain but nourishing food, saving my money, washing my neck and ears, allowing myself two small drinks each evening before my frugal meal.

In a word, I trapped myself.

During the winter I had arched many a bottle over into Pat Patterson's yard, just a fifth's throw away, by instinct I suppose. Feeling, perhaps, that I ought to have a little insurance. Pat kept throwing them back. As many gamblers are, he was a teetotaler, and he didn't want a lot of bottles popping up in his yard. As a pitcher, Pat could have got a job with the Brooklyn Dodgers. He hit my iron trash barrel every time, usually very late at night, frightening me almost to death. When he no longer could see the barrel because of the deepening snow, he hit the side of my cabin, which was worse.

I was not entirely responsible for all these bottles; after all, I am not a full-fledged alcoholic—every time I try to be one I run out of money. Many of these bottles belonged to Willie Kuhrtz. He would come over to see me, lugging a bottle in which there was about one-half inch of whiskey. "Well," he would say, "this time it's on me." After one drink Willie would be astonished that the bottle was empty, and I would have to fish my own reserve from behind the British battleship curtain in the bathroom, and start losing money. I always was left holding Willie's bottle, and would have to do something with it.

Throw it into Pat's yard. After all, it certainly wasn't mine.

One day I mentioned this to Pat.

"Look," he said, "I'm sorry to have to throw those things back, but in my profession if they see a lot of bottles in my yard in the spring I could lose my job. They think I'm drinking and would give a dude an even break in a poker game, by accident. On the other side of your cabin, there, is the athletic field of the God damn high school. Throw your extra bottles out there."

A hunch, if I ever heard one.

Now came a crisis in my life, and it was Pat to whom I turned. Berry wrote that instead of coming on in May she had changed her mind and was leaving New York in two weeks, which would bring her to Jackson in mid-April.

Zounds!

At the time I got her letter a gentle snow was falling, and the yard looked beautiful, but I knew that beneath this false smile lay a pattern so firmly embedded in the basic ice and the icelike snow that I never could cope with it, in time, unless I had a bulldozer, and I did not have one. I took a walk around the yard, in the new thin covering of snow, and was tripped up several times. I ended in Pat's kitchen, explaining my problem.

"We can get a certain number of bottles out of there," he said, "but the best way to make them look fewer is to make other things look more, so help me, I'm a son of a bitch if it isn't. Now let's just take a walk around my premises, here, and see what we can find."

Between his trash barrel, his yard, and his cellar, we found nearly a hundred cans that had contained spinach, string beans, succotash, beets, peas, and other items that women keep thinking are food. Pat was very fond of graham crackers and similar junk, and we found thirty or forty empty boxes, most of them in Pat's kitchen, as he had been saving them for starting fires.

"They look too new," Pat said. He poured a pound of coffee into his dishpan and filled it half-full of water and boiled it. He soaked the cracker boxes in this to age them. He then stepped on some of the cans, and squashed some of the boxes. Then we planted them in my yard, meantime taking out as many of the bottles as we conveniently could manage, without leaving holes in the ice, which would seem ostentatious.

When Berry arrived, everything was in order.

But the result mixed failure with success.

Delighted at what appeared to be a change in my choice of food, my finally leaning toward what she always had thought was best for me, she began to come home from the store with large bags of this idiotic junk. I ate as many graham crackers as I could manage, then, survival being the first law of nature, I broke down and told her the truth.

We had a good laugh over it.

"The only thing that disturbs me," she said, "is what is happening to the younger generation. Wilford had an editorial in his paper last week, about that. I think he's right. The high school kids are drinking. They found a lot of bottles in the school athletic field. I don't like it."

I then told Berry, and later Wilford, the truth about that, withholding nothing.

Those bottles, I explained, had belonged to Willie Kuhrtz.

chapter 23

My Cold War with Clover Sturlin

THERE are funnier and easier ways of making a living than clowning for the rodeo. At every rodeo, whether it's in Madison Square Garden or Jackson Hole, there is a clown, and the clown seems to be having the time of his life and—as the case is with respect to other forms of clowning—the Republicans in the audience get indignant when they hear he gets paid for it.

But the work of a rodeo clown is about as deceptive as a job can be. In a word, it is the only dangerous one in the arena. Apparently out there to make the spectators laugh, to provide a change of pace from what appears to be the constant peril of the riders, he picks up his share of the dough for attracting the attention of angry Brahma bulls, loose broncs, and other frustrated animals that have just got rid of their tormentors, to his own person. Away, that is, from the often prostrate cowboy, who may have had the wind knocked out of him or is suffering from bruised feelings.

The crowd roars as he scales the fence about six inches ahead of a pair of eager horns or a flock of flying hooves, or dives into his barrel in mid-arena just in time to fool destiny. It's all very funny, strictly a pratfall exhibition, evidently, but the clown is the most finely trained, most expert individual on the premises.*

* Bob Crisp recalls the time at Madison Square Garden when the clown got hurt and Homer Holcomb, a bronc rider from Idaho, volunteered to take over. A Brahma bull with Pete Kercher, a Wyoming cowboy, on top, came out tough and tossed his rider and went for Holcomb, who was waving a

Clover Sturlin was one of the best clowns in the business. Although he never made the Garden, his services always were in demand throughout the Western rodeo country. (Rodeo riders, by the way, often ask who the clown is going to be before signing up.) Before taking up clowning he had been a top rodeo contestant, and before that he had been a fine cowboy—still was. He came into Jackson Hole in 1924, driving a Model T Ford that had no brakes, a circumstance he made up for by cutting down a lodgepole pine and dragging it behind the car as he made the steep descent down Teton Pass in order to ride in a local rodeo. He took saddle-bronc money and later returned, in a car that had brakes, to live.

He retired from competition when, as he says, "The saddles began to get too small for me," and went into clowning. Some years later, with the start of a family on his hands, he bowed to his wife's wishes and quit this for less hazardous work. He got a job in a small local sawmill and the first day he was there a splinter of wood struck him in the left eye, blinding it.

For years, now, Clover has been in the wood and coal business in Jackson. When Berry and I rented a house there in 1938–39, one of the first things that had to be taken care of was the wood supply: quaking aspen for kindling and for a hot fire in the kitchen range, lodgepole pine for the heating stove. Dick Winger told me to see Clover. I looked him up and after some discussion I ordered two cords, one of each kind of wood, to start with. I asked him how much it would be and he said eleven dollars a cord.

"That's a hell of a lot of money," I said.

Clover looked at me steadily with his good eye and thought it over. "It's a hell of a lot of wood, too," he said slowly and went away.

---

blanket. Holcomb got mixed up and instead of getting out from behind the blanket as the bull charged it he moved the blanket to one side and stood there naked and took the bull on his chest and was in the hospital for five weeks.

But when he brought the wood, a few days later, it didn't look like such a hell of a lot. Berry, whose father once had been a timber cruiser in northern Minnesota, his success in buying stumpage depending on his accuracy in estimating the board feet in a stand of pine, cast a semiprofessional eye on the wood and didn't think it added to two full cords. She said I ought to speak to Clover, in a nice way.

"Clover," I said, next time I saw him, "how does a fellow go about measuring a cord of wood, unless it's cut in four-foot lengths?"

"Experience," he said. "Having only one eye, I have to look at it twice, and I'm usually a little over, but that doesn't worry me. Live and let live. Speaking of wood, there's no need of your going to the trouble of telling me when you need more. I know that place you're living in, and I know the stoves. Leave it to me. You'll need twelve cords to winter it, and I'll see you don't run out." *

This sounded extremely sensible, so I agreed.

The next delivery, a cord of mixed aspen and pine, came in the midst of a blizzard, the snow deep on the ground and getting deeper. Clover came in for a cup of coffee after he had unloaded, and we passed the time of day. After he had gone, Berry went out to look at the wood, and when she came in she was disturbed.

"Dear me," she said, "that's an enormous amount of wood

* The people who take care of you in Jackson do not like to be told what to do. Once I got a can of plums from Mercill's store, along with other things I had ordered. "Good for you at this time of year," a note on the slip said. Once Berry wanted some new shelves in her kitchen, and I looked up Bill Blackburn, man of all work. He looked the kitchen over, investigated our pantry, lifted the cover of a pot of stew on the stove, and shook his head. "You don't need any new shelves," he said. "You hardly got enough grub to fill the ones you already have." He went away. Later, in October, we were awakened early one morning by a pounding on the wall of our log house. I went outside, and found Bill Blackburn chinking the logs. I suggested that I hadn't asked him to do this. He jerked his head toward the mountains. "Snow coming down," he said. "I know when to chink the logs. You think I'm some kind of a God damn fool?"

for just one cord. What did you say to Clover that time you spoke to him?"

"Nothing," I said.

"I don't know," she said uneasily. "Are you sure you didn't hurt his feelings? I like Clover. I think Clover is nice. I hope you didn't talk him into cheating himself."

I went out and looked at the wood and it did seem an awful lot, just as Berry had said. The next time I saw Clover, I bought a drink to weaken his resistance and said, "Clover, that was an awful lot of wood to be called a cord. I didn't mean anything by that little remark I made a few weeks ago. You got to remember, you're in business. You got a family."

"Oh, hell," he said. "A few extra sticks, here and there, never hurt anybody. It's all between friends."

A few days later, upon using up the last of the original two cords, I started work on the new delivery: stack pine chunks in the woodshed, split aspen for the kitchen and arrange it neatly beside the stove. The blizzard had gone, it was a bright, clear day, not too cold, and I whistled softly as I worked, in sheer joy of living.

As I went along I noticed that the woodpile flattened out and got smaller rather quickly. The reason was not hard to come by. Each piece of wood not only was covered with a great deal of snow, but this snow, or most of it, was bound to the wood by a coating of ice. Often I would put a piece of aspen on the block, to split it, only to find that by the time I had trimmed it of snow and ice it didn't need splitting after all: it was small enough for the stove just the way it was.

I told Berry, "I don't think Clover cheated himself too much on that wood."

As the winter went on I noticed that he showed up with his loads of wood either during a snowstorm or right after one. "Clover," I said to him one day as we sipped a hot one against the chill, "you've hit a very good average on that wood. One stick of wood to one-half bushel of snow and ice. Do you soak the wood in water before you roll it around in the snow or do you just depend on the storm you always deliver it in to take care of that?"

Instantly I could see that I had injured Clover's sensibilities.

He placed his drink carefully upon the bar. "Well, now," he said. "Well, now." He speaks very slowly and deliberately. "Well now, why would I want to do a thing like that? I deliver the wood in bad weather because on nice days I'm out cutting. When I figure the load I always allow for the snow. Why, you yourself said those cords looked awful big. You thought I was cheating myself."

"I know it," I said. "Please excuse me, Clover."

"Another thing," Clover said, "a little ice and some snow on the wood never does any harm. Slows it down just right to keep a fire all night. No use burning the place up. Look at the way John Dodge does it. He cuts a lodgepole pine about twenty foot long and shoves it in through the window of his cabin and into the door of the stove. As the wood burns, he pushes the log that much farther into the stove. Just to save himself cutting up a trunk of lodgepole into stove lengths. The way it is with you, you get your wood cut up ahead of time, with just enough moisture built right into it to keep the fire at the right temperature. Otherwise you'd be getting up all night putting fresh wood in the stove and spending your money right and left. Take it back in the cities, you have to pay plenty for an automatic gadget like that."

I thought it over. "I appreciate it, Clover," I said. "Thank you very much."

Clover picked up his drink and finished it and ordered two more. "On me," he said. "Well, I estimated twelve cords for the winter. Now I tell you what I'm going to do. I'm going to dump a cord in your yard, there, without charge. Then . . . Let's see, how deep is that snow?"

"Around two feet, on the level," I said.

"Okay," Clover said. "I'll dump that cord, then in the spring, when the snow is gone, although you'll still need wood, I'll throw in another cord, or whatever it takes to get you through. I said twelve cords and I meant twelve cords. No hard feelings either way. Is she a deal?"

I said she was a deal.

When the snow went down in the spring—or the ground came up, as many old-timers claim—and the awful skeleton of our winter was exposed to us, among other things that emerged was a record-breaking crop of firewood, this having nothing to do with what we thought was our only woodpile. It was scattered over a considerable area.

Berry and I stood there looking at it. "Well," she said, "that's the answer. We have cheated Clover again. He brought us a free cord because you complained, and here it was under the snow all the time. And he's going to bring us some more, to make up. You better go see Clover."

I found him at the Cowboy.

"Clover," I said, "I owe you an apology, to say nothing of the price of a cord of wood. And you won't have to bring us any more on your guarantee to get us through on twelve cords. We found a cord and a half, nearly two cords, when the snow went away."

Clover nodded. "I know it," he said. "I thought that when the snow went down you might find a stick or two, here and there, that you didn't know you had. I'm used to that. I always allow for the snow, like I told you."

"In any case," I said, "I owe you for that cord."

Clover laughed a little and winked his good eye. "Not at

all," he said. "Not at all. Forget it. What's a few sticks of wood between friends? A present from me to you and Berry."

I felt uncomfortable. "I can't have you lose on the deal," I said.

"I won't," he said. "I figure you'll be here next winter. A satisfied customer. I'll come out all right. I always have, so far."

chapter 24

Victory in the Sun

WINTER now lies helpless in the gutter, bleeding to death as its colorless lifeblood follows every track, crack, crevice, ditch and gully, just so it points downhill. Some of it may find false sanctuary in hoofprints and footprints and cellars and stagnant pools, but over the landscape as a whole it flows in ignominious defeat.

Once formidable, dangerous, in contemptuous power, arrogant in its solid state as ice and snow—packing the old one-two punch, the ice tripping you and the snow sitting on you—this dreadful season now finds itself beaten by the simple law of gravity, and the harder it weeps in its agony the faster it runs away.

Listen to the babble of the liquid snow and bits of rotting ice that swell the small valley streams——

Nearly had you nearly had you nearly had you . . . nearly had you . . . We'll be back we'll be back . . . we'll be back . . . we'll . . . ahem! . . . be back. We'll . . . whoops! . . . be . . . back . . .

And expiring on the bosom of the overloaded Snake River, swirling and tumbling toward the Pacific, the erstwhile tough guy snarls in a sideways Brooklyn accent——

WAIT TILL NEXT YEAR! . . . WAIT TILL NEXT YEAR! . . . WAIT TILL . . . NEXT YEAR! . . .*

* The wonderful, incredible news has just come in over the ticker. Happiness reigns in my home, and, I am sure, in other quarters all over the joyful land, including a certain remote cabin up Buffalo Fork, inhabited by Frenchy. The Dodgers won the 1955 World Series! Great catch by Sandy Amoros,

Okay, we'll wait, chum, but right now things are looking up, thank you.

Hit him again, May!

It's your turn now, dear.

We've had it.

Although the delicate light green of the baby leaves of the quaking aspen marbles the hillsides in a pattern accentuated by the deep green of the spruce and pine, the little park in the town square, a captive barometer, more intimately reflects the emergence of the community's spring.

The park is a relatively new thing. It began life as a gully, or depression, which was a part of the main north-south game trail through the valley, as I mentioned in a previous chapter. The first buildings were put up on either side of this, and it was used as a kind of town dump. Later this was filled in with earth. As the places around it increased in number and the square began to take shape, a few hitching rails were put up and finally these became a single rail fence, forming an enclosure, or nearly one. This was used as a corral or resting place for transient horses or cattle being driven through, and as a very dusty or very muddy town common, as New Englanders would call it, from which small boys came home in deplorable condition after a game of one-old-cat.

The fence itself served as a tying-up place for saddle horses, pack outfits, wagons, mail and passenger stages, and, as time went on, an object for automobiles to edge up to. In 1932 the Federal Government asked all states to participate in a George Washington Bicentennial program aimed at civic improvement. Wyoming, in common with many other states, chose the establishment of town parks as its contribu-

terrific pitching by Johnny Podres. So, instead of "snarls in a sideways Brooklyn accent," the above should read, "the erstwhile tough guy suggests, in the cultured Groton-and-Harvard English favored in the penthouses of the New York Yankee advocates, that another season, old boy, impends."

tion and hired a park and landscape specialist to cooperate with the various communities. In due time he got to Jackson, cased the joint, planned the park, specified the trees, and left a blueprint.

No funds were provided from outside, so Mildred Buchenroth, wife of Bank President Felix Buchenroth, set out to raise the dough. (I never can understand why bankers should have to "raise" dough. They have a huge safe chock full of it, haven't they?) The thing was accomplished, the members of the town council, headquartering at the RJ Bar, did all the physical labor required, and the park started to show signs of life.

Oddly enough, the trees and shrubs that were specified by the state expert, and subsequently were bought, did not include a single species native to the region, which, of course, is lousy with foliage. There were tall Russian and Canadian poplar, Colorado blue spruce and laurel willow for shade and stateliness, and honeysuckle, lilac, Cotoneaster, wild black currant and crabapple for arrangement in the middle and the corners. Plus the hedge, which remains unidentified. However, looked at in perspective, there is nothing especially paradoxical about this circumstance. Nothing really is native to Jackson but Jackson itself.

Under the expert and loving care of Stewart Reynolds, whose fingers are all green thumbs, in charge of it since 1936 and still there today, in 1955, the park grew up, and after these years it is a splendid thing.*

* Much of the original hitching fence that surrounded the place still is there, although now hidden in the hedge. Other parts were demolished by automobiles poking their noses into them. In 1938 a much sturdier fence was built, four feet outside the old one, to handle the brunt of the automotive impact. But Detroit stepped up its armament and in 1941 a third fence was put up to protect the second one. In 1950 this had to be protected by an outer rampart of logs two feet thick, bolted to each other and to cross-members, fourteen inches in diameter, lying upon the ground. This gives the park, today, a formidable demeanor with respect to its outer defenses.

In winter, as we have seen, it is a lively place. The community Christmas tree rises from its middle, and there the chill throne of the Queen was built. The departing and returning warriors of the Cavalcade paraded around it, and it served as a background for the great snow-statue contest.

In summer it is a cool green haven for persons in love, or nearly in love—just as the little doe nestled there in the snow night after night to drink in the beauty of the great buck deer—and it serves people who are sleepy and have no place to go, for cowboys down on their luck, and for casual strollers, that vanishing race.

In a sense, of course, it is a hothouse plant, a foreign thing, but it's fun to watch it bloom.

So all through the valley the feminine hand of resurgent spring lies gently on the land, bringing new life in many directions. It is calving time in the home corrals and the cowboys are busy branding new citizens who soon will accompany their mothers to the high summer range, where later they both will be joined by their husbands and fathers, looking toward still another spring to come, for the work of a woman is eternal, the distant slaughterhouses sharpening their knives . . . The elk, too, with such calves as they have managed to save, walk slowly, rib-thin, back to the heaven of the lush grass, leaving their winter-killed behind them.

The coyotes, giving up dreams of a cocktail-waitress steak for this year, move sorrowfully back to the tall timber and common grub . . .

The Forest Rangers are opening remote cabins, the Park Rangers dusting off their lantern slides and oiling their mimeograph machines against the closing of school in New York,

---

Unscrupulous bartenders and other opportunistic guides have been known to tell innocent tourists that the park originally was a fortress for protection, not against the onslaughts of the Buick, but against those of the Sioux.

and the dude wranglers are preparing for the harvest soon to come. In a word, the Hole now is expanding, from Jackson outward, slowly, while in town the summer business establishments and other facilities are being made ready, and one of the more hardy of the lady shills, vanguard of the office-party survivors, can be seen in silhouette on the horizon, ready for another shot at the dudes . . .

The soil is being tilled.

Hay and alfalfa are being planted by the Government people, looking toward next winter's influx of the elk, and by the ranchers, for wintering their cattle, and in town the people are making little gardens, and here Rudolph Rosencrans, one of the pioneer Forest Rangers of Jackson Hole, now old and blind, plants his larger garden to a crop he never will see, but that he will put up in hundreds of glass jars during the summer for distribution to his friends.

John Dodge, the man who invented the idea of thrusting a trunk of lodgepole pine through his cabin window and into the stove, to save sawing it up, now cultivates his 20-acre field, doing his part. He sits on a sulky plow, drawn by two mules. A lover of poetry since his college days in New England, he starts the mules, then drops the reins and opens his volume of poems and spends the morning reading, aloud. He lets the mules go wherever they want to go, pulling the plow in circles, figure eights, or any other didos they have in mind.

Dick Winger comes along. "John," he says, "why don't you plow your field the way other people do, in regular furrows, up one side and down the other?"

John lifts his nose, temporarily, from his book.

"Well," he says quietly, "the whole field has got to be plowed, hasn't it?"

Which about wraps it up:

The whole field has got to be plowed.

chapter 25

I Will See You in the Morning

NOW THAT spring is here to stay—apparently—there is still another drift of people into Jackson Hole, and into Jackson. This may be called, I suppose, the return of the natives, for it is made up of local residents who went away last fall to escape the rigors of winter or for other reasons pulled out, sometimes with the ringing proclamation, "forever!"

Among the first to return are the horse wranglers, those who supply pack and saddle horses for the dude and tourist trade, hunting parties, even for some of the cattle ranchers. They had taken their strings of horses and a few mules out of the Hole last October or November, driving them to winter pastures in eastern Wyoming, Idaho, Montana, in some cases to Utah and Arizona. Unlike cattle, horses will scratch for their own feed in winter, supposing the snow cover to be thin enough. Since this condition does not exist in the Hole they are taken out to lower altitudes where they can find grass on wind-swept ridges and in other areas where the snow is light.

Ike and Jack Neal have the largest string, forty animals or more, that they drive over Togwotee Pass and the Continental Divide to the lower Dubois area, while Helen Davis takes her small bunch of eight saddle horses and two pack mules clear up to Ennis, Montana, a 203-mile drive that takes her nine days to make.

Helen is one of the first to leave in the fall, and usually the first to come back in the spring, following a route down through part of Montana, across a piece of Idaho, then over a Forest Service mountain road into the Hole and to Noble Gregory's pasture and corral a few miles from Jackson. Then, her charges taken care of, she leaves them with Noble for a few days and stays in town, relishing the relaxation of four walls and a real bed after her nights in a sleeping bag on the trail. She visits friends, handles a few drinks of bourbon and plain water, may play a few hands of poker, before going on to her summer work, then into the hunting season, for she is a licensed big-game guide.

It's rather curious, I think, how Helen came to be interested in horses. At the age of twenty-one, in 1935, living with her parents (her maiden name was Helen Head) in Marshalltown, Iowa, she was found to have pulmonary tuberculosis and was sent to a hospital in Casper, Wyoming. In five months she was convalescent and the therapy prescribed included mild outdoor exercise, such as riding. She fell in love with her therapy, virtually at first sight, stayed on for some time, then her father took her over to Dubois, where she slept outdoors, rode more and more, and helped wrangle horses. In 1940 she came on to Jackson Hole.

She got a job handling horses with a dude oufit at Signal Mountain, a tourist attraction in the Hole, and nine years later, having built up a string of seven horses of her own, plus a dozen she rented from Ike Neal, she got the concession for herself. Meantime she had married Jack Davis, a good cowboy, and with him had driven forty-eight head of horses and mules to Green River City, Utah, for wintering. They sold some to Indians en route, and bought some, or traded, and in the spring started back with more than they had taken out of the Hole, then ran into a terrific blizzard in southern Wyoming, lost more head than they had gained, and just barely got through it alive.*

After running the Signal Mountain dude concession for a while, all by herself, shoeing her horses and otherwise taking care of them, taking up to eighteen riders to the top of the mountain and back each day, she dropped it in favor of handling fishing and hunting parties down in the Hoback. She breaks her own broncs, giving no edge to any cowboy in Jackson Hole, and always takes two pounds of candy with her when she starts out for Montana.

She cares nothing for dudes—"They won't listen to anything you tell them, because they feel they have enough money so they automatically know about everything, even if they never saw it before"—and she likes her horses because they are not intelligent and need care—"They are only as bright as you would expect a horse to be. In other words, dumb, for such a big creature." (Attaboy, baby!)

Her registered brand is PDQ. She tried to register various brands, when she started out on her own, but every one was turned down by the State because it was too close to something else. Finally she wired Cheyenne: MUST HAVE BRAND PDQ. They said PDQ was okay with them. It's a hell of a brand to handle, but it's all hers.

The winter travelers and sojourners-out begin to show up, from various directions. Jess Wort saw a fellow in India throw a rope into the air and a boy climb it and both disappear. Another fellow there would ask him to think of a card, just *think* of it, without even looking at the deck, and he would

* Jack and Helen no longer are married. He is as phlegmatic a cowboy as I ever saw. Once when he and another chap were putting up a fence Davis inadvertently placed his right hand on top of a post just as his companion was hitting it with a maul. He looked at his badly smashed hand. "Confound it," he said, "I believe I have made a mistake."

throw the deck at the ceiling and your card would stick to it. Jess, no slouch with cards himself, saw terrific possibilities in this and offered the Indian a wonderful job in Jackson Hole, but it was refused . . . Bill Everett saw a man wrestle an alligator in Florida, and in a side show there was a boy with six fingers on one hand . . . Retired merchants and cattle ranchers, and some still active, return from sitting out the cold in the vapid bubble bath of California, and the dude ranchers come back from New York and San Francisco with summer bookings in their pockets . . . Cowboys come in from the winter rodeo circuit . . .

Now we come to those rebels who, only last October, had shaken the dust, mud, snow, slush, and ice of Jackson Hole from their boots "forever," this often preceded by loud public speeches. A scattered few actually make it stick, astonishing everybody, but those who show up in the spring, hoping nobody will notice them, add up to a greater number, for Jackson has a strange fascination for those who once have been granted her favors.

Even John Wort, who with his brother Jess now owns the beautiful Wort Hotel, within which is encased that elegant exhibit, the Silver Dollar Bar, some years ago joined those who decided to leave forever. Johnny took a snag of steers over The Hill to the railroad, then to Los Angeles. Having sold the steers for a nice pocketful of money, he stepped out a bit, met a lot of interesting people, and ended without any dough. He made what he thought was the decision of a lifetime: he never would return to Jackson. It was entirely too small, when compared with Los Angeles; it was even smaller when compared with the great wide world. The hell with it. Somebody at the stockyards told him he might get a job at Peter Jackson's private polo field, a very fancy layout, at Santa Barbara. He hitchhiked up there and was taken on as a groom and exerciser of the polo ponies. At first he liked it, but people kept snapping their fingers and calling him "Boy!" and he had to keep saying "Yes, sir!" without snapping his fingers, from morning till night, and this wasn't what he had had in mind, so when he had enough money he returned to Jackson Hole.

He returned, however, with a deadly purpose:

One day he was going to go back to Santa Barbara and he was going to play polo with some of the richest people in the United States of America, and he was not going to say "Yes, sir!" again as long as he lived, to anybody.

John made it, on both counts.

First he painstakingly raised himself a modest string of polo ponies. He crossed thoroughbreds with quarter horses and came up with something pretty good. This took him a few years. When he had just what he wanted he took his string down to Santa Barbara. By this time all concerned had forgotten that John was the "Boy!" who had exercised their horses for a short spell some years before, and he was invited to show his ponies. He did so, riding them himself. He never had played polo, but his uphill-downhill-through-the-willow-thicket cowboy technique, later to be brought to even fancier circles by Eric Pedley, of Texas, fitted polo like a mallet glove. He was invited to play on one of the teams. He did so and was, in a word, sensational. He was asked to exclusive clubs, but never went: "I was just a common Wyoming cowboy, and I knew where I didn't belong," he told us.

John's horses made a hit, and he deigned to sell some of them. Now he not only was a polo player, he was in business. After that he raised more polo ponies and went down every year, for a while, to play more polo. In the spring he would come home without any ponies, but with his pants pockets full of lettuce.

He made his last trip in the fall of 1950. He had eleven ponies. Just before he was due to leave, the deer-hunting season came on and some friends of his wanted to go out and get their bucks. John made up a party. The trouble was, they were short of pack horses, so he took along his polo ponies and used them for bringing in the deer. He had to blindfold the nervous, high-strung creatures before packing them, so they couldn't see what was going on. A few days later he left for California with them, in trucks. I haven't seen John since, but I understand he came back in the spring, again without any ponies, but that was that; he quit while he was a winner. Later he went down occasionally to see his lovely daughter, who attended a private school at Santa Barbara, and to see friends, but no more polo.

Henry Westerhoff was another who left Jackson Hole forever. He came to this country from Germany after World War I, having been an infantryman with the 21st Reserve Division, Fifth Army of the Wehrmacht, a trouble-shooting shock division sent in to stop break-throughs and otherwise to handle battle areas in distress. It was expendable, subject to terrific casualties: after Henry's company had been reconstituted three times at Verdun he was the only one of the original outfit still living. Along with many thousands of his comrades, he was successful in surrendering to the Americans in the closing days of the lost war. They all tried to surrender to the Americans, because they knew that our troops had better food than the French or the English had.

The Germans liked both the Americans and their food—"If even the soldiers have food like that, what a country it must be!"—and Henry decided to come to the United States both for these reasons and because he wanted to get as far away as possible from the horror he had known. He managed to get on a quota in 1923.*

* When he went through customs he had a bottle of brandy under his coat. When he leaned over to fasten his suitcase after it had been passed, the bottle slipped out. Henry was horrified, for this was during Prohibition and

In his search for peace and quiet he drifted westward, arriving in Jackson Hole in 1929 after a friend had described it to him, explaining that there wasn't even a railroad there. He got a job as chuckwagon cook and general ranch hand, and around his cabin on Squaw Creek built up a herd of tame deer, in the company of which—they all but shared the cabin with him—he found further sanctuary from mankind's violence, and relief from his memories of it.

Then came World War II, and Henry, now a citizen and proud of his prerogatives as one, made the mistake of declaring, in his heavy German accent, that we should not get into it. He was not concerned with the issues involved, whatever they were, only with the soldiers. But we did get into it, and Henry, caught in the hysteria of the moment, was looked at by some as being at least an unpatriotic American, by a few as virtually a traitor, even as a possible German spy.

He lost his job. He strongly felt that his friends were embarrassed when he appeared among them, and he sensed a tension, an ominous quiet, when he entered a group. So one day he packed his belongings in his pickup truck, said goodby to his deer, and left the place he loved, forever.

He got a job in an Oregon lumber camp. One night two years later he went to town with some of his fellow lumberjacks to see a movie. The movie was a Western. At one point in the action a wide corral gate was opened to allow some horses to leave the enclosure. As the gate swung, in a smooth and perfect arc, Henry half stood up in his seat and slapped his knee in delight.

He knew that gate well, for he had hung it himself. It had been a tough one to hang because he had had to set the post in a

he knew that it meant instant deportation. He explained to the customs man that his little group had planned on drinking it in celebration of their arrival —"A toast to your country." The customs man looked it over. "Very good brandy," he said. "Perhaps you ought to put it in the suitcase, where it won't get broken." That cinched the United States, for Henry Westerhoff.

solid rock formation—guying it with wire cables—and although it had swung free at the time, it was sixteen feet long and heavy, bringing a terrific leverage to bear, and he had been afraid it would sag later. Now he knew that it had not.

The movie people had come into Jackson Hole to film part of this Western picture, and had chosen the corral as part of the background.

Henry Westerhoff got up and started out.

"Where you going?" one of his friends asked.

"Home," Henry said.

He walked out of the theater, returned to the camp, packed up, and without even waiting for his paycheck drove back to Jackson Hole. When he got there he made an interesting discovery. Apprehensive upon arrival, afraid he might still be an embarrassment to his friends, he found that people wanted to know where the hell he'd been. They said, in effect, "You seemed to like it so much here, and suddenly you disappeared."

Most of what he thought had happened to him had been in his own mind.

He returned to his cabin on Squaw Creek, where, had his deer not been teetotalers, they would have tossed a cocktail party for him.

One pleasant October day Art Chapman, a fine cowboy, on the quiet side personally, like Bob Crisp and Bill ("Breathless Love") Howard, announced, in the Silver Dollar, his impending departure for Egypt, where he would spend the rest of his life. Willard Miner asked him what was cooking in Egypt, and Art was obliged to skip the details. He had been reading something or other, and he knew a fellow who had been there, and it was the land of opportunity, and he was on his way.

He left the following day with his bedroll and a suitcase

and that was the end of Art Chapman until he returned in the spring, having shook the dust, not of the valley of the Nile, but of Needles, California, from his boots.

About a week after Art left for Egypt, Jack Yokel parked his truck outside the Silver Dollar and came in, with a flourish, to say goodby to everybody and everything. He was going to Alaska, lock, stock, and barrel, to begin a new life. His horses and a few other things were in the truck. Jack ordered drinks for the house. As new customers came in, he extended the invitation. Among those to enter was his father, Mike Yokel, and Jack bought him a double one and they touched glasses in a final farewell.

I had known Jack since he was a little tot. His father had taken up a homestead near the post office of Wilson, at the foot of Teton Pass, eight miles west of Jackson. He was a young man then, newly married. Unfortunately the homestead he picked out was just about the worst one in the whole valley: rocky formation, no bottomland for raising hay and wintering cattle, among other things. The going got tough, and Mike had to turn to his previous profession for cash money, to make ends meet.

He was a wrestler by trade, and this was in the days when a wrestler really was one, not a comedian: a bout was a sports event, not a circus for the edification of elderly ladies taking a refresher course in anatomy, the answer of the Ladies' Aid to the charms of the female perfectionists of Hollywood. In order to wrestle, Mike of course had to go outside, spreading his services from Chicago to the Pacific, and he was very good, always in demand. He was a middleweight, and although I think he never held a national championship, in the United States, he certainly held many state and regional ones.

Mike never stayed away any longer than necessary, which meant that he had to keep traversing that Hill, and since the wrestling season was in winter, and in winter The Hill was an uncertain proposition, he often had to make it over into Idaho, to the railroad, on snowshoes, and back again—a little more tired, perhaps—on the same snowshoes.

At this time Mrs. Yokel began to have children, and now came one of the most curious races in the history of competitive sports. The more Yokels the more Mike had to go out and wrestle, and the harder he had to try to take the winner's end of the purse. By the time his wife had given birth to half a dozen youngsters, Mike was going over The Hill and coming back so fast he was practically a blur: the Jackson's Hole *Courier* had such a hard time keeping up with him that upon occasion it found itself announcing his departure, his victory, his return, and the birth of a new Yokel, all in the same issue.

Eventually, having pinned to the mat the shoulders of so many strangers that he lost count, and began to lose work, he turned to Australia. His absences now were longer, some of them lasting the whole winter, or summer, seasons being what they are below the equator, and the *Courier* got less mixed up. He won, and defended many times, the middleweight championship of Australia, and retired at the age of forty-four, undefeated abroad, and with ten fine children at Wilson, six girls and four boys. His ranch later worked out very well, he bought other property, and today is in the real estate business in Jackson Hole and doing fine, thank you, a jolly fellow, surrounded by enough children, grandchildren, and friends to rival the elk herd itself in sheer numbers.

So Jack Yokel kept swinging an arm to include everybody at the bar, telling Willard to fill them up.

Many toasts were drunk to Alaska. Or, of course, bust.

Jack left the Silver Dollar in an exit worthy of the late John Barrymore, shouting goodbys to Jackson Hole, got into his truck, and drove away.

It seemed quiet in the bar, without Jack. Willard Miner

was the first to recover. He struck the bar a mighty blow with his fist. "Son of a bitch!" he said. "God damn it, Jack forgot to pay for all those drinks!" He grabbed the slip from beside the cash register and handed it to Mike.

Mike glanced at it and handed it back. "He'll pay you," he said, "as soon as he returns."

"But he left for good," Willard objected.

"He'll be here," Mike said patiently. "April, maybe May. No later." He took a deep breath. "They drift out, they drift back. Le them see the world, or whatever part of it they can, while they're young. Jack will pay you for the drinks in the spring, Willard. Save the slip."

Willard wiped the bar. "If this town needs a slogan," he said, "I've got it for them."

"What is it?" I asked him.

Willard thought it over, briefly:

"Goodby forever; I will see you in the morning." *

* The following is quoted from the August 4, 1955, issue of Floy Tonkin's bright new weekly, the Jackson Hole *Guide:* "On Sunday morning under the guidance and experienced navigation of Jack Yokel, two guests of the Fish Creek Dude Ranch were successful in negotiating the rapids of the Snake River canyon in a rubber boat . . . Never been done before . . . Jack Yokel, an experienced river man with a vast knowledge of the Snake, is probably one of the few men in the valley who could navigate such a trip."

chapter 26

Social Notes (May)

The Croquet Court

PAT PATTERSON is getting things ready for his summer guests, the lovely shills and waitresses who soon will begin to appear. His first concern, now that the frost is out of the topsoil and the grass is showing, is the croquet game. Soon the wickets all will be in place, the terrain carefully raked and smoothed over, new grass seed sown in places where it is needed, brilliant colors painted on the balls and the mallets and those sticks at each end of the court, or playing field, or whatever the name of it is.

When the summer-long tournament starts, Pat will put in his orders for a watermelon a day with the grocer, for eating beneath the tree at noon, everybody invited. The sound of gay laughter, interspersed at the proper intervals with the delightful, high-key noise of bitter and always illogical quarrels, will drift in through the open window of my cabin, adding charm to my day.

The only blot on the landscape is Pat's outhouse, or, as it often is called, privy. It is just south of the croquet layout, and directly in my line of vision when I want to look at the mountains. During a snowstorm this is all right, because the roof of the thing is peaked, and blends into the general blur of my view—many times, underestimating the depth of the storm, I have looked at Pat's privy and have confused it with the Grand Teton. But now, in the spring, no more snowstorms, the privy stands there like—let me see. Like an outhouse in a fog.

"Pat," I said one day, "you never use that thing. It just stands there, rotting away. I'm terribly tired of looking at it. What do you say we set fire to it?"

Pat was adamant.

"It has a certain sentimental significance," he said. "What would a home be without it? Everybody ought to have one, even if he has two bathrooms in his house, to remind him of his youth and to impress upon him the fact of the blessings he now enjoys. I'd burn down my home, here, before I'd burn that thing down. I can't understand your even suggesting it. I don't know where you were brought up. If I did what I really want to do, I'd move it right in to where the croquet court is now, a place of honor, by God, son of a bitch if I wouldn't, so help me, and plant a flower bed around it. Back in Iowa, where I was born and raised, we always had a small woodpile between the privy and the house, so that if the hired girl would start for the privy, and somebody would be looking, she could pick up a couple of sticks of wood and bring them back to the house. Once when we had some guests out from the city I rigged up a pull-chain, the thing they were used to in those days, attached to a cowbell on top of the privy, and they would pull that chain just from habit and ring the cowbell and they'd stay in there for fifteen minutes before they had the nerve to come out. So help me."

For a professional poker player, Pat had a soft spot in his heart. Deep inside, he was a sentimental man.

Another Libation

I went over to Riverton to visit Paul and Patricia Petzoldt on their homestead for a couple of weeks and immediately upon returning I checked in at the Silver Dollar to see what

CHEW-SMOKE
MAIL POUCH
Live—!
with LITTLE
LIVER
PILLS

had been going on. When a person is away he alway thinks great changes are taking place back home, but upon his return finds that nothing much has happened.

"Well, Willard," I said, "I had a fine trip."

Willard looked at me. "You been away?" he asked.

"Riverton, to see Paul and Pat Petzoldt," I said. "It was mentioned in the Social Notes in the *Courier*."

Willard shrugged. "Dews has been away, too," he said. "First time he's been outside in twenty-two years. John Wort had to drive to Rock Springs and Dews hitched a ride with him and went on a vacation. He came back this morning, so I've heard. I haven't seen him yet. He'll be in."

The only other news that Willard had was that the Yankees were leading their league in the young baseball season, and the Dodgers were ahead in the National. Frenchy had been in with his furs and had left twenty dollars for Willard to bet for him on the Dodgers to win the pennant. Willard was disturbed about it.

"I hate to see Frenchy throw away his money," he said, "but if by some miracle the Dodgers should win, and I have kept his money for him instead of betting it for him, I'm out twenty bucks. It's a hard thing to decide."

In a few minutes who should enter but Mr. Dews. He was dressed up: tweed suit, striped tie, tie pin made from the $1 gold piece, shoes shined, city-type hat placed tastefully upon his head. Everything but gloves and cane.

After the greetings were over, Mr. Dews invited us to join him in a libation, and we did so.

"Well, Dews," Willard said, "the Yankees are three games ahead already, and the Dodgers just lost two in a row to Pittsburgh, of all people."

"The Dodgers will take the World Series," Mr. Dews said with firm conviction. "In any case, however it is, you won't disturb my morning sleep with that baseball bat this season.

I am moving"—here Mr. Dews paused a moment for maximum dramatic effect—"into a new apartment. I have leased a spacious room in the rear of the barbershop, completed the deal just this morning. Adjoining my apartment is a large zinc tub in which Harry washes his towels and things, which will serve as my bathtub. In that space also is running water, hot and cold, just a step from my door, and a heating stove with a flat top, upon which I can prepare a hot meal."

Willard thought it over. "What will you do for beer?" he asked.

Mr. Dews stiffened, and, for the first time since I had known him, seemed to be at a loss. "Why," he said, "I'll . . . just as usual, I'll buy it here at the bar. Why . . . ah . . . let me see. Why do you ask?"

"Cheer up, Dews," Willard said. "You'll still have charge of the stock, down there. In fact, it needs some work right now. You better get out of those clothes."

"Willard," Mr. Dews said, savoring every word, "I am still on my vacation. It ends at six o'clock. I have a few more things to do." He turned to me. "You repeatedly have invited me to visit you in your domicile during the winter, and I never got around to it. Will you be home in a matter of about an hour?"

"I'll be waiting for you," I told Mr. Dews.

Mr. Dews sat down and placed his feet upon the Central Disposal Unit and while I was preparing a libation told me about his trip. He had visited old friends in Rock Springs, where he had worked as a cigarmaker, a gambler, and man about town for some years. He had had a plate lunch at his old roominghouse for fifty cents. Then on to Salt Lake City by bus to see other old friends. Many were gone, a few still were there. One of them owned what Mr. Dews described as one of the largest and foremost jewelry stores in the city.

He showed me his friend's business card. Across the top of it was printed LOANS MADE ON ARTICLES OF VALUE.

He also had a letter, which he had found awaiting him in Jackson, from Challenger Airlines. This was addressed to Mr. C. Walter Dews and said, "We notice in the 'People About Town' column of the Rock Springs Rocket a brief news item concerning your activities. May we suggest that in your various trips through the Intermountain area you will find it speedy and convenient to use our service. We trust you will make it a regular habit."

After I had read the letter Mr. Dews folded it carefully and put it away in his inside coat pocket.

"You have a fine, cozy place here," he said. "A splendid apartment. Better than mine. But when I get settled, I want you in for a visit and a libation. I notice Pat's grass is coming up fine, for the croquet game. Lots of people around town have got lawns, of late years. A modern development. But I still say a lawn is a foolish thing. No character to it, no strength. In order to get rid of a lawn all you have to do is turn your back on it for a few minutes and the next time you look it isn't there. Grass is a city thing, like a crowd going to Ebbets Field to see the Dodgers beat the tar out of the Yankees next fall, it all bends in the same direction and each blade holds up the other blades. Dandelions begin to grow in the lawn, each one by itself. You try to get rid of them, but they come back. Sometimes a big weed grows there—the old saying, growing like a weed—and nobody knows where it came from. It has no family, no relatives, just grows by itself, and in the fall it dies and is blown away, tumbling dead across the fields, no home for the winter, but in the spring it pops up, somewhere."

Mr. Dews finished his drink and I made another for him and another for myself.

"The weed is native to Jackson Hole," he said. "Whether

it's a plant or a man. Going into the animal kingdom, it's just like a tumblebug, which ought to have some other name, because a tumblebug, if you've ever watched one, never tumbles except when it's trying to climb uphill. Curious thing. It never gets there, some bird comes along and gobbles it up, but it keeps trying. It's not afraid. There's no sense in being afraid. My mother told me never to be afraid, and I never have been. Not even of death itself."

One more libation, and Mr. Dews took his feet down from the Central Disposal Unit, complimented me on the arrangement of the interior of my cabin, and left.

He stood in the doorway for a moment, looking at Pat's croquet layout, now nearly ready for use, then stumbled over the steps that Willie never had repaired for me.

He lifted an arm, and I lifted one, and he walked away in the direction of his new apartment.

The Last of the Old West

Jackson Hole proudly calls itself The Last of the Old West. This is printed on dude-ranch folders, on official town stationery, on commercial and private letterheads, and on banners, such as the one Roy Jensen fastened to the top of his Cadillac at the time of the Cavalcade. If there is one place in the West that calls itself The Last of the Old West, there must be at least thirty. It's almost as bad as the number of communities in the United States, supposing them to have a hill two hundred feet high, that loudly bill themselves as "The Switzerland of America."

Jackson Hole is no more the last of the Old West than I am, or than you are. But it has one thing to its credit: the Old West died, if it ever died anyplace, in the very middle of Jackson Hole at high noon on May 3, 1943. In that connotation, Jackson Hole is the champ.

Early in 1943 President Roosevelt set aside a part of the

Hole, adjacent to Grand Teton National Park, as The Jackson Hole National Monument. (This since has been added to the Park.) This area, as it happened, was directly across the path of the spring cattle movement from the lower Jackson Hole ranches to the summer range, beyond. Word got around that the Federal Government would not allow cattle to be driven across the Monument. This was true of other National Monuments and it was assumed that the rule would apply here. The Park Rangers and other federal people, it was rumored, would line up at the edge of the Monument to prevent passage. The local Park people, with supporting word direct from Washington, assured everybody concerned that the cattle could be driven across the Monument, but the cattlemen chose to ignore this.

The Jackson Hole people were divided about the Monument, half being in favor of it, the other half bitterly opposed to it. This latter half was made up mostly of cattlemen and their adherents, and they evidently thought their cause would be lost if they actually were allowed to cross the Monument. It would, as the saying is, take the wind out of their sails.

So they got ready for battle.

A few years before this, Wallace Beery, a movie actor who specialized in Western tough-guy roles but with a tear ever trembling in his eye as he lifted prop scalps from prop Indians, had been the star performer in a picture called *Bad Man of Wyoming*, much of which had been shot on location in Jackson Hole. He fell in love with the place, bought a few acres of land on Jackson Lake, and built a nice lodge there, for summer use.

When five ranchers pooled 653 yearling Herefords for forced movement across the Monument and into the summer range, come what may, Wallace Beery galloped into the picture, mounted on a borrowed white horse, equipped with a scabbard containing a .30-.30 Winchester rifle. Mr. Beery wore the same big black hat that he had used in *Bad Man of Wyoming*, and I think some other blood-and-guts Westerns. He had his picture taken, and it was reproduced, with the Tetons in the background, on Page One of Section 2 of the Salt Lake *Tribune*.

The yearlings were gathered in Spring Gulch, just outside of Jackson, at Cliff Hansen's home ranch, on Sunday, May 2. The following morning the embattled ranchers, with their town colleagues, gathered in the Elks' Hall to check firearms and distribute ammunition and make speeches. (The *Courier* had come out three days before with a streamer, THESE MEN MEAN BUSINESS! !)

The order of the day, promulgated by Mr. Beery, was "Shoot to Kill!"

While the meeting was being held, the Herefords got restless, and the ranchers' wives, who had been holding them in place while the menfolk were girding their loins, decided to start the drive. The steers were taken upcountry by the ladies. When they reached the boundary of the Monument, nobody was there, so they just kept on going, and crossed it.

Upon hearing this, the men in town threw caution to the winds, as they say, loaded their guns and ammunition into automobiles, and sped to the scene. The ladies, by this time, were on their way back. Somebody, among the battalion of determined heroes led by Mr. Beery, had thought to bring along a few cases of beer. So all concerned now sat on the bank of a small creek marking the boundary of the Monument, and threw empty beer cans across it, each toss accompanied by loud imprecations directed at the Government of the United States, as personified by the Monument.

Then they went home.

Thanks to the bloodthirsty Mr. Wallace Beery, and to

Hollywood as a whole, a new slogan for Jackson Hole, "The Last of the Old West Happened Here," was thought by some citizens to be in order.

The Scar on the Mountain

Now I shall have to go back, again, to the days of my first residence in Jackson. It was this same month of May. One morning a whole side of a mountain flanking the Gros Ventre River slid into the canyon, choking it: a million or so tons of earth and rock, thousands of trees, one of the largest landslides known, in the eyes of man, in the Rocky Mountains. The huge scar, a mile long and half a mile wide, in the shape, roughly, of a cross, has been seen by a few million tourists, who do not know what it is.

Guil Huff had that beautiful ranch at which Jimmy Simpson and I had stopped on our ride to Crystal Creek. Guil was out rounding up a few horses and some cows when he saw the trees on the mountainside above him go into a crazy slow-motion dance, and he heard a deep rumble, and he turned toward home and rode as fast as his horse would take him. The mountainside came down fast, and sometimes he was only a few feet ahead of the bouncing boulders and the trees, now tumbling head over heels, but he made it, then got his family out in time.

The slide formed a great dam, and the river began to fill in back of it and built up a lake. When it got just so deep, it floated Guil's house, his barn, and his outbuildings from their foundations, and they drifted around in the lake. Guil had salvaged what he could from the house before the water was too high, but now he had an idea he could get into the upper loft of his barn, where he had stored a few things.

I went along with him. We got a rowboat from the Forest Service and went out to his floating buildings, and I held the skiff steady while he got into the barn loft and he came back with some skis, two pairs, then with some snowshoes. That was all he could find.

It was a very hot day, one of those things that can come along, especially in a river canyon, even in Jackson Hole, and in May at that. We had come up in a Model T Ford and had left it a half mile away from the Forest Service rowboat, and now we had to carry the snowshoes and the skis to the car, on a narrow dirt road.

When we were almost to the car, soaking in our sweat, two other cars came along, toward us. They were filled with people plainly intent on a sightseeing adventure. They honked their horns, and Guil and I stepped aside, into the ditch. But now they stopped. They plainly were dudes, the first arrivals of the season at some dude ranch in the Hole. An extremely beautiful babe, sitting next to another extremely beautiful babe, in the first car, leaned out toward us.

"How's the skiing and snowshoeing?" she asked, and went into a fit of laughter. She turned to her friends. "Look, kids, they're out skiing. Get a load of it, please. I told you about the natives around here. Isn't it lovely? They're looking for some snow, on a day like this, for Christ sake! What you won't see!" She looked back at us, smiled ingratiatingly, and the cars went on.

I got kind of sore, but Guil, who had just lost everything he had in the world, with no hope of salvage, the work of a lifetime up to then, took it in stride.

"Forget it," he said, grinning. "Those are just dudes. They don't know anything. They can't help it; it's the way they are. They've come in early, and they'll enjoy their summer here with us. They're really nice people."

chapter 27

Farewell, My Fancy!

Concerning the departure of the last lingering cocktail-hour guest, at dawn . . .

I HAVE left Jackson Hole, specifically the town of Jackson, several times, but never unless I had to. That is to say, my flirtation with this sweet babe has many points in common with some of the Jackson Hole citizens' flirtation with the rest of the world. They leave Jackson, apparently for good; I go there, hoping it is for good. They have to come back. I have to leave. No fair.

Berry and I have lived there together three times; four times I have gone in alone. Since we seem to be living in New York at the moment, and were not born in Jackson Hole, I figure that the exits must have exactly matched the entrances. Our inevitable departures, either both of us together or me alone, always have been based on considerations financial in nature. This circumstance, in turn, stems from—rather, really is—an occupational hazard of my trade, which is that of a free-lance writer.

The theory is that a free-lance writer can work with equal success, or lack of it, no matter where he happens to be, and this is true of really good writers, especially fiction writers, the number of which roughly is comparable to the number of shortstops who can go into the hole after a grounder and make the long throw, at the same time competent enough at the plate to hit .250 or better against major league pitching, especially the low outside curve. This has nothing to do with me. My work is journalistic in nature, which means you have to wander around, like a coyote on the trail of a cocktail waitress, in search of sustenance.

Sustenance is a nuisance.

One of these days Berry and I hope to find a lean-to that doesn't leak too much and faces away from the wind, beneath a tree that grows chocolate ice-cream sodas and uses rum for sap, keeping us both happy. But so far this has been nothing more than a lovely dream.

I have spent more winters in Jackson than I have summers. In spite of the dramatic beauty of the Hole in this season, summer more or less bores me. Nearly every time I have gone in I have hit the cocktail hour right on the nose, as a result of calculated design and fiendish purpose. It seems much more sensible to me to sit in a nice bar, a hot rum handy, and wait for your friends to drop by—and everybody in the Hole will do so if you can sit there long enough—than to shag them all over the landscape. In a general way, and this includes such things as the descent of the elk herd, the October–April (or May) segment of the year is the interesting one. Everything is concentrated; the integrated movement of the season, the people, the animals, is right there before you. A heart-warming time, in spite of the cold.*

The first time I left Jackson was in 1925, when I went over the Hill with Clay Seaton and the preacher. I was going back to Chicago to make some money (joke) and when I told Dick Winger why I was pulling out—Berry and I even had moved our furniture in, that time—he asked, "What do

* Winter is especially charming when you don't have to get out into it, of course, beyond brief exhilarating tours of the town square. There is rather a difference between looking at the view from the picture window of the Silver Dollar and having to get out into the view and feed the cows. Many in Jackson Hole feel that speaking of a charming winter roughly is comparable to speaking of a charming murder.

you want to make money for?" I said just because I did, the same as anybody else, and he said, "Most people want to make money so they can retire, and according to insurance statistics they want to retire so they can travel. If you should do that, where would you travel to?"

I knew he had me trapped.

"Here," I said.

"You are already here," Dick said impatiently.

It's hard to explain that sometimes you have to go someplace else to make enough money so you can stay where you are, and in spite of Dick's crushing logic I went away, and have been going back ever since, trying to make it stick. My last pitch was in 1948–49–50, when I tried twice, one sustained struggle lasting fifteen months before I was decapitated.

Oddly enough, the only time I went there for just a short visit, not intending to stay, I remained for a year and a half; then when I decided to make it permanent, I had to leave. Upon having to leave, I just barely got away without having to stay forever.

This was in 1938. Berry and I and our son, Sherwood, started from Chicago to Hollywood, where I was to look for work, in a small Ford car loaded, or rather partly loaded, with all our belongings. We decided to go around through Jackson Hole to visit friends and to get in a little trout fishing. We figured on staying no more than a few weeks.

But I lost our traveling money—in other words, all our money—trying to get rich playing roulette, which complicated matters. A year later, still there, we decided we might as well carry out our 1925 plan and settle down for life, never mind Hollywood, let them eat cake.

But this silly "sustenance" thing caught up with us and Berry and Sherwood drove up to Minnesota to dine with our parents, eating on an uninterrupted basis for a while, while I was to go on to Hollywood, as soon as I could manage it, to see what I could do there.

But now, for the first time in my life, I couldn't get out of Jackson. No dough. I had to stay on, getting along the best I could, through nearly all the following summer. Pat Patterson kept me supplied with trout, I ran my credit where I could—an inexorably narrowing beam—and accepted such invitations to dine out as I could manage to wangle. Once I had a windfall: Doc MacLeod gave me a hind quarter of bear. I hung this in the little cellar under the log cabin we had rented from John Wort and it was wonderful. Presently it began to get maggots on it, but I discovered that these all were on the outside and I could cut them away and come to good meat. Even *better* meat, for by now it was aged and tender—you nearly had to eat it with a spoon.

One night, looking at my watch to see what time it was—I don't recall the reason for wanting this meaningless information—I noticed that my timepiece was made of gold. I decided on a final try at the tables. I got thirty dollars on the watch, and started with roulette. I won a little, and shifted to the poker table, which Pat Patterson was running.* Playing with me were two young cowboys. Others drifted in and out, but the three of us stayed with Pat. By dawn we were broke and went outside and sat on the board side-

* Pat always won from me at poker, but once I dealt a hand of stud to Pat and Sheriff Olin Emery that still is referred to in a kind of awe. I don't deserve any kudos, as dealing (unless Pat was doing it) required no skill, just passing out the cards. I dealt Pat three fours showing and Olin had a possible straight or flush coming up. The betting was plenty. The final cards were a fourth four to Pat and one that seemed to fit Olin's hand. Pat apparently had a cinch, but Olin, amazingly enough, raised his bet. They raised back and forth and finally Pat called. Olin had a straight flush. Neither ever had seen this situation before in a nothing-wild five-card stud game. Olin, raking in his money, swore he'd never arrest me again as long as I lived, and he never has. Pat, though, didn't speak to me for three days.

walk. One of the boys had a sack of Durham, and we rolled cigarettes and looked at the pink sky.

The cowboys were just passing through Jackson, on their way to Nevada, hitchhiking. I invited them over to my place, where I had part of a can of coffee, a couple of cans of tomatoes, and of course the bear. We ate some of both and went to sleep. Jim Jackson, one of the boys, had a saddle blanket, a saddle, a braided horsehair lariat that he had made himself, and a large elkhorn pocketknife. During the days that followed he sold everything but the saddle, one thing at a time, and we kept eating, even after the bear meat had been buried in a shallow backyard grave.

They stayed with me a couple of weeks, then Jim got a job in the Hole and decided to stay on, and his companion—I can't remember his name—got a hitchhike and went on to Nevada.*

One day Arthur Welch, a friend of mine who had a summer cabin down in Hoback Canyon, came to town and I saw him at the Cowboy, where I was running a beer on the cuff. He was leaving early the next morning for Los Angeles, by car. He invited me to go along. We discussed my situation. He would finance me for the trip and he knew where I could get a room in Hollywood, with kitchen privileges, for very little money. I decided to go.

All I took with me was my typewriter and a suitcase. Everything else I owned I left behind in lieu of rent, or rather as part payment thereon, and we went down to the Hoback in

* These two cowboys are the prototypes of two similar lads, called Hade and Steve, about whom I later wrote a number of fiction stories for magazines. Four movies were made from the stories, and I saw one of these on TV not long ago. Incidentally, isn't it curious the number of times the name "Jackson" has emerged in this book? The Hole was named after a Jackson, the name of the tour impresario who stranded the schoolteachers at Turpin Meadow was Jackson, the polo field at Santa Barbara was owned by Peter Jackson, and now along comes Jim Jackson, the cowboy.

the late afternoon. Arthur had invited some neighbors, including my old friend Vic Sottong, in for a few drinks, in celebration of his leaving for Los Angeles. After a couple of drinks I noticed that the sun was setting, or perhaps just had set, I couldn't see from the little gulch in which Arthur had his cabin, and I was feeling very low about leaving Jackson Hole. I knew I could see at least the lower part of the Hole, if not the Tetons, from the top of a hill that rose just beyond the cabin. So I took a Scotch and soda with me and climbed it.

The hill was steep, and it was high, steeper and higher than I had thought, but I made it. I sat on the summit and looked back up toward the Hole. The sun just had set, but the sky was pink and yellow and there was a light-blue haze in the part of the Hole that I could see. I felt like a perfectly silly fool (which I certainly was), sitting there drinking my drink, trying to swallow it past the lump in my throat, and I remembered all the people who had come up through here so many years ago: Colter, snowshoeing alone, unknowingly on his way to discover the tortured earth—"Colter's Hell"—later to be known as Yellowstone Park, darling of the schoolteachers; and Jim Bridger, pioneering his way through the Wind River range and discovering South Pass, the gateway to the Pacific Northwest through Jackson Hole; and David Jackson himself, the trapper, and many others: then the homesteaders coming in over the Hill with wagon wheels lashed to the flanks of their horses . . .

I could imagine them, in the course of their bitter and often discouraging struggle, asking each other, "Why are we doing all this?"

And one clear voice came through:

"So that one day some ass can sit on the top of that hill over there and drink a Scotch and soda."

Net discovery: the cocktail hour.

Finishing my drink, I now for some reason or other decided to make a little fire, as a farewell gesture. This was a bald hill, no trees, just some sagebrush and greasewood, and I picked up a few dry sticks and placed them on a rock and lit them. Presently I had a very modest little fire, and I sat beside it in what by now was darkness.

Somebody began to shout, down below, and soon I could make out the words—

"Put out that fire!"

I didn't obey at once, and now I heard at least two persons coming up the hill. They were puffing and swearing and I could hear loose stones rattling down behind their scratching boots.

"Okay," I called down, "I'll put out the fire," and I put it out very quickly. They kept on coming anyway, and one had a flashlight and I recognized two U.S. Forest Service Rangers. They were from a station down the Hoback and I hadn't seen them much, just enough to know who they were.

They were angry. They looked around for sparks that I might have missed in putting out the fire. "For the love of Christ," one of them said, "what the hell do you mean, making this fire?"

"I was signaling to the Indians," I said. "A secret ritual. I'm quitting the Hole at dawn. However it is, I'm sorry; I didn't mean to trouble you. Were you down at Arthur's party?"

"No. We saw the fire from the highway. We were on our way to the movie in Jackson. Now we can't make it in time."

Feeling like a worse fool than ever, I apologized all the way down the hillside, but there was nothing I could do about it now. When we got to the cabin we found the rangers' wives inside, having a drink. The trip to Jackson to see the movie, now that they were late, was abandoned.

Howard Willard

I apologized all over again, but nobody paid any attention.

"What was the movie?" I asked one of the wives.

"I don't know," she said. "All I know is that Olivia De Havilland is in it. She's beautiful."

Suddenly I remembered where I was headed for. Jackson Hole was behind me, Hollywood ahead, and in this split second I crossed the divide.

"Miss De Havilland is indeed beautiful," I said, in a professional manner, instantly adopting the judicial tone of the established expert, "but in my opinion she is not a first-rate dramatic actress."

At this point Vic Sottong handed me a fresh drink and I took it, but the glass was slippery and I had a wet hold and it dropped to the floor. The floor was of rough planks. The glass hit it squarely, bottom down, and it stayed that way. Not a drop spilled over.

Everybody else was astonished, but I managed to take it in stride. I knew that I had to, for to me it was a symbol, a farewell and a portent, in a single glass of Scotch and soda. The cocktail hour in Jackson Hole was over, at least for me, and if I could remember how I had dropped this glass, to make it do what it had done, or if I could have the same incredible luck, if I could bring it off even once in three tries in Hollywood, testifying to my genius and my skill—not a drop spilled—I not only would get a job there, but in a few years I would own it.

About once a year I get a letter from Jim Jackson, one of the two cowboys who stayed with me in my cabin. The letters always are interesting; when I see his handwriting on the envelope it pleases me very much. At one time he is in Nevada, rounding up wild horses in the hills and selling them, next he is foreman of a ranch; suddenly he is in the tall timber of northern California, a lumberjack; he is a U.S. Marine, on M.P. duty in San Francisco; at last he is married, has three kids, is back in Nevada on a ranch of his own.

His letters never are long, for he is a man of few words, and the final sentence never varies:

"That is all I have to say, so will close."

Okay, Jim; same here.